Endurance:
The Blog of a Distance Runner and Triathlete
Part I – The Boston Marathon

Ben Ingram

Copyright © 2014 Ben Ingram

All rights reserved.

ISBN: 0615946224
ISBN-13: **978-0615946221**v

DEDICATION

To Kendra: you have been through a lot, taught me a lot, and put up with a lot.

ACKNOWLEDGMENTS

Thanks to my parents for always supporting me in my running and writing. Thanks to all my coaches, teammates, even those who I only ran with once or twice. Your spirit is in every page of this book.

MONDAY, SEPTEMBER 22, 2008
WHY DO I WANT TO WRITE A BLOG ON RUNNING THE BOSTON MARATHON?

1) It will help me focus on my training and five me a reason to keep running long miles through the cold winter.

2) I'm in the health field and I want to develop some running related material for a possible future web based running community.

3) I've been running competitively for 19 years and I still can't quite answer the question I had the first time I toed the line when I was in 7th grade; "Why am I doing this?" Maybe this blog will help me answer that question.

TUESDAY, SEPTEMBER 23, 2008
GOALS

For any athletic event that's seven months out it's best to have multiple goals. There are so many unknowns that it would be crazy to say "If I don't run Time A I won't be happy."

I have four levels of goals;

Goal A:

Run sub 2:30. My PR is 2:36 – so, this might seem a little beyond what I'm capable of doing. However, I've run 10k and half marathon times that point to a capability of sub 2:30. Still, you might say, "Boston is a hard course. Maybe you should save that goal for a flat course." That's true – but, people have run decent times at Boston, I live in a relatively hilly city (Baltimore) for training, and I have a good training group. Basically, you never know when you'll have a chance to run a good time. Yes, I will need to follow my training to a "T", no injuries allowed, no bad weather on race day etc. I know I can do this at some point – why not now? At least I think I can. Probability it will happen? I give myself a 5-10% shot.
Everything would have to go right and I would have to run a sub 1:10 half in my tune up race to even attempt it. That being said – most of my training will assume that this is my goal pace.

Goal B:

PR. This is quite a bit easier, but still difficult. I ran a 2:37 last year in NYC and I'm not getting younger (although many runner PR in the marathon into their mid-30's). I'd say there's about a 50-60% chance that I'll get goal B.

Goal C:

Finish without completely blowing up. Although I could get goal B or even A while also blowing up (my definition of blowing up is running at least two miles at 30 seconds slower than goal pace) it's not likely. The marathon is so cruel because it can make you go from feeling the most fit in your life to crippled in a few hours. Leg muscles cramp up, range of motion disappears, basically your body can fall apart until you only march on because you're not sure how else you can get to the finish line. I've run four marathons – I've felt like this in three of them. So, I give myself a 25% chance of not blowing up.

Goal D:

Finish. Even when I've felt awful I've been able to finish. I've never dropped out of a marathon and I"ve never injured myself so badly that I couldn't get to the starting line (knock on wood). I would say that there is at least a 95% chance that I'll be on the start line next April and finish.

WEDNESDAY, SEPTEMBER 24, 2008
THE TRAINING PLAN

I'm going to use a combination of training plans from Pete Pfitzinger (Advanced Marathoning) and Jack Daniels (Daniels' Running Formula). They both have plans that have four phases. The Pfitzinger plan is a little simpler – but I like some of the workouts in the Daniels book a little better.

I'm planning on writing extensively on what these books say about distance running training. I'll probably bring in some theory from a few other books I have laying around too.

The plan will run for 24 weeks. I'll get into the details in a later post.

FRIDAY, SPETEMBER 26, 2008
MARATHON QUOTE #1

"You have to forget your last marathon before you try another. Your mind can't know what's coming." - Frank Shorter

I completely agree. In three out of four marathons I've experienced complete physical breakdowns. I'll tell you a little more about those good times later.

Why am I doing this again?

PHEIDIPPIDES

There aren't many sporting events that I can think of that are based on a story from an ancient Greco war and named after a battle in that war. Pheidippides was, of course, a messenger from the Athenian army. The story goes that after the Athenians were victorious over the Persians at the battle of Marathon Pheidippides ran the 26 miles back to Athens to announce the victory. He made it back, stated "we have won", and died on the spot.

Not exactly a story that one would think would lead thousands of people every year around the world to try and equal his feat. I did a little reading on the internets – and the factual history around his run is a little shaky – but more historically firm is the fact that he ran to Sparta to request help in battling the Persians before the battle of Marathon. To reach the Spartans and get back to the battle he ran 150 miles in the two days BEFORE the famous 26 miles. No wonder he died – he didn't taper properly.

MONDAY, SEPTEMBER 29, 2008
2:03:59!

Wow!

I kind of felt sorry for Geb at the Olympics last month. One of the greatest runners of all time was limited to basic pacing duties for his countrymen in the 10k. But at the end of the race he had a big smile on his face even though he didn't medal. Maybe he knew something the rest of us didn't.

Haile Gebreselassie is one of those mythic men of running. At the age of 35 he runs the first marathon under 2 hours and 4 minutes. His first world record was the 5,000 meters in 12:56 and change in 1994. Think of that – he's been setting world records for 14 years! That's incredible.

Also incredible is his range. The difference between 5k and 42k is quite a bit and yet he's been the best in the world at both distances and everything between. The man has had a movie made about him (Endurance, 1999) which was actually pretty good.

He has two Olympic gold medals and eight world championships for indoor and outdoor track. Pretty much an overall stud. In terms of range and length of career he is probably the greatest distance runner of all time.

To put his marathon pace in perspective – there are only 15 Americans who have ever run faster than one hour 2 minutes for the HALF marathon. That's sick.

TUESDAY, OCTOBER 3, 2008
GODS AND MORTALS

Like Pheidippedes, most early distance runners were messengers. They were so important that even a god of Greek mythology, Hermes, was given the role of messenger. The need for messengers was mostly related to how bad the roads were in most parts of Europe. As any competitive person can imagine, races between messengers probably started with bragging by one or the other about their exploits. By the end of the 18th century the occupation of foot messenger had pretty much died out, but foot races, especially in Britain, went on.

The first races in the 17th and 18th centuries were usually sponsored by pubs. Like boxing, gambling was the main draw for spectators. Also like boxing, the men who raced were mostly from the lower classes. However, by the mid-19th century schools like Oxford and Cambridge were fielding cross-country teams. Their affiliation made it a "respectable" sport. However, there was a distinction between pros who ran for money and the amateurs who ran for fun. This split is why the Olympics was only for amateurs at the beginning. They wanted the event to have a more "noble" atmosphere than could be found at most professional races. Given doping issues that track has now – maybe they were on to something.

I took most of the historical information in this post from the book "Lore of Running", by Tim Noakes, MD. At over 700 pages, it is THE text book of running – as in, you wouldn't want to read the whole thing unless you were going to be tested on it.

TUESDAY, OCTOBER 7, 2008
THE CRUEL HAND (FOOT) OF FATE

I was in my hometown of Ann Arbor this last weekend. I don't get home much other than the holidays or a wedding/funeral – and then usually not for long. So I tried to see as many people as possible. One friend who I was looking forward to seeing was my old high school friend Todd Snyder. Both because he has a six-week old little girl and because he was supposed to run the Chicago marathon next week. I'd heard through the grapevine that his training with Hansons (an Olympic development running group) was going incredibly well. The rumor was that he had been training for a 2:13 marathon. That's pretty much within spitting distance of making the Olympic team.

So, after making the obligatory comment on his newborn (actually she is very cute of course) I asked him about whether the rumors were true. He said that training had been going great until last week. He had some pain that had been developing in his foot - and now it was so bad that he couldn't run. They hadn't done a bone scan yet – but the doctor thought that it was a stress fracture of one of the bones in his foot. Todd was his usual positive self – saying that the training had given him a lot of confidence about what he could do in the future, but it had to hurt – to get so fit and then not be able to show it.

I have to admit that at first my disappointment was more about the fact that I was going to have to wait awhile before he was anointed the next Brian Sell and I got to brag about beating him in middle school. But then it made me think about how dedicated these Hansons guys are to run 130-140 miles a week – giving up their lives for several years to chase down a dream where so many things can go wrong. But I guess that seemingly random cruelty of the marathon is, in a perverse way, what makes it alluring.

SUNDAY, OCTOBER 12, 2008
RECOVER WEEK 1 OF 3

As I was watching the Chicago marathon online this morning there was a small part of me that thought it might be "fun" to jump in the Marine Corps marathon in a few weeks. Falls Road Running Store has at least on free race number. But I quickly regained my senses – the next few weeks should be all about rest. Soon enough I'll be running long miles. Running a marathon right now – no matter what the pace – is not a good idea.

The Baltimore half was a little brutal yesterday. I placed well (4th dude) – but it was a little slower than I had hoped (1:14:44). But those hills are no joke and I was basically alone (other than passing marathoners) for 11 of 13 miles. I'm not too sore today – but I'm glad that next week will be basically off. I'm ready for the break mentally and physically. I'm going to do some more weight training and yoga in the next few weeks. So even if I'm not running much I'll have some physical activity.

MONDAY, OCTOBER 13, 2008
MY FIRST MARATHON

It was a bright March day in Los Angeles. I was two weeks short of my 25th birthday and about to run my first marathon. I was long on confidence and short on experience. I thought that running 25 laps in college on the track meant that I was tough enough for anything. I was wrong.

The first hitch wasn't really my fault. Somebody called in a bomb threat – so I stood around with 20,000+ people as the sun steadily warmed the air for 45 minutes. I probably should have taken that as a sign that someone was telling me to reconsider my plans for the race. That maybe I should take it easy, given that I hadn't really run over 16 miles in training.

Once the gun went off I felt the exhilaration of running with thousands of people. I was only a few years out of college and hadn't really run a race with that many people. There is a release of energy that occurs at the start of a race this large – unfortunately I would need that energy later.

In the first few miles I just floated along – we started to enter South Central LA and I can remember high fiving kids. I was thinking, "this is easy!" Then I saw the lead female pack. I moved up to them pretty easily and then stayed in the pack for a little while. It was fun to think I might be on TV. Then for some reason I decided they were going too slowly – so I opened up a gap on them. This was about 10 miles in and I still felt great.

Things soon changed. At around 14 miles I remember coming up over a rise from a bridge. I spit to my left – only to realize that I had spit on the lead woman who was overtaking me. I mumbled an apology – but all I was think about was "I'm starting to hurt and I still have 12 miles to go – crap."

The wheels really started coming off around mile 16. I was completely overheated. The temp was around 70 degrees and the California sun was relentless. I don't remember what my water stop strategy was – but I think it was probably the potentially life threatening "drink when you're thirsty."

I remember finally seeing a water stop – like an oasis in the desert – around mile 17. I was so thirsty that I stopped completely – I drank water and poured it all over myself for several minutes. I head sirens in the distance – I was sure they were coming for me.

When I started up again I realized that stopping for that amount of time probably wasn't the best idea. Most of the muscles that I needed for forward locomotion were completely cramped up. It was like learning to run all over again. My brain knew what my legs should do – but my legs had other ideas.

There was one thought that kept spooling around my head – "I really want to quit – but I don't know how else to get to the finish line."

A few other memories stand out in my head – trying and failing to catch a guy who looked like he was pushing 200lbs; saluting an American flag (I'm not particularly patriotic); and generally cursing my own existence. It's amazing how quickly one can go from slapping hands with strangers to feeling like a cripple. That's what the marathon does to you.

I finally did finish. Thank goodness that my parents were there. My mom had agreed to drive me back to San Diego where I lived. I'm glad she did – because I was in the back seat curled up in the fetal position for the two hours back to SD.

So again – why am I doing this?

WEDNESDAY, OCTOBER 15, 2008
QUOTE - ZATOPEK

"We are different, in essence, from other men. If you want to win something, run 100 meters. If you want to experience something, run a marathon." - Emil Zatopek

Zatopek was one who like experiences and winning. In the 1952 Olympics he won both the 5,000 and 10,000m gold medals. At the last minute he decided to run his first marathon as well. He got the gold medal in that too. As great as Bekele is – there is no way he could have won all three in Beijing. Part of that is how competitive all these races are these days – but part of it is how incredible an accomplishment it was by Zatopek.

I'm not sure I completely agree with this quote – because most of us who competed on any level ran long distance only because we weren't fast enough for a more "sane" distance. But the quote does illustrate why you see thousands of people lining up to run marathons – not 100 meter sprints. We are all looking for a unique experience. Something that is challenging and maybe even a little dangerous.

SUNDAY, OCTOBER 21, 2008
PERIODIZATION BY MESOCYCLES

Don't fall off your seats folks – I know this sounds exciting. Periodization is basically the concept that to run our best we need to have different types of training throughout the year (including rest). Both Pfitzinger and Daniels prefer 24 week "macro cycles" to best prepare for a goal race. Both authors break the 24 weeks down into four training mesocycles (Pfitzinger's term) or phases (Daniels' term). This is not completely ground breaking – everyone who has run on a track or cross country team has trained using some version of these cycles. I'm going to quickly summarize each of these cycles today – at some later date I'll go into each one in more depth.

Phase one is simply running "easy" mileage to build an aerobic base. This base building is important so that you can increase mileage without increasing intensity. There are many benefits to easy running on the cardiovascular system and even at the cellular level. I might do some strides during this phase as well, which helps with running economy.

Phase two introduces some quality training – but not too much and not too intense. Along with some threshold workouts, I'll include strides after an easy run and hills.

Phase three is the most intense phase. It includes both intervals and threshold runs – as well as more marathon pace runs (if that's your goal race). The goal is to stress the systems that will be tested in your goal race enough to strengthen them without getting injured or burned out. It is this thin line that you have to play with. You have to really listen to your body and focus on hydration and nutrition to ensure that you are replacing the liquids, carbs, protein, and vitamins/minerals that your body is using at a high rate. There might be some racing during this phase as well.

Phase four is the last phase of quality training. You want this to be as specific to the event as possible. If your goal race is hilly than you want to train over hills – if it's going to be warm then you want to train in the heat. This phase also includes the taper in the few weeks before the race. This is critical because your body is able to recover from the training without losing much fitness. Tapering is a tricky balance as well – but usually it's best to error on the side of too much rest. My PR marathon came after I hurt my knee in the month prior. I used a stationary bike mostly in that last month of training. Rest is much more important than most people realize.

Speaking of rest – there is a rest phase, which I'm in the middle of right now. Rest doesn't have to mean no running whatsoever – but it does mean a major reduction in mileage and no hard running. The transition between my rest phase and phase one will be gradual – but the basic length of each phase is as follows:

Rest phase: 4 weeks
Phase one: 4 weeks
Phase two: 5 weeks
Phase three: 9 weeks
Phase four: 5 weeks

So , it's basically a 27 week plan with 23 weeks for the four main phases.

TUESDAY, OCTOBER 28, 2008
THE BEGINNING OF MODERN TRAINING: ARTHUR NEWTON

A book I've mentioned before, Lore of Running, dedicates an entire chapter to the contributions of Arthur Newton. Newton raced in the 1920's and 30's. He was what we would today call an ultra-marathoner. He ran a large number of races between 60-100 miles – but more importantly, his ideas helped to modernize training for all distance runners. In Lore of Running, Tim Noakes identifies nine "rules" of Newton's training that have become "common sense" in long distance training.

1) Train frequently year-round. Before Newton, most world class runners only trained part of the year – and not very strenuously by today's standards. In fact many books of the time suggested walking as good training.
2) Start gradually and train gently. Since many runners didn't train all year long they tried to get back into training too quickly. Newton praised the benefits of what we would now call long slow distance (LSD). Noakes defines LSD as 20-25% slower than race pace.
3) Train first for distance (only later for speed). I would say that's the major feature of my training for Boston. I'll be doing quite a bit of distance before I ever hit the track.
4) Don't set a daily schedule. Well, I've kind of messed up on this one. My days are scheduled for the next 25 weeks. However, I know I need to be flexible. If something comes up or I'm too tired or the weather is crazy on a "quality" day – I have no problem in postponing the workout.
5) Don't race when you are training, and run time trials and races longer than 16km only infrequently. This basically relates to the idea of "periodization" discussed in a previous post. Set aside a good chunk of time that's just for training – not racing. Now, his

idea of "infrequently" is a little different than mine. He suggested that marathoners should not race more frequently than every two months – running a marathon about every two years is enough for me!

6) Specialize. Noakes interprets this as make sure that you train for a specific distance. Training for a 5k is very different than training for a marathon. Another way to think about it is to concentrate on the distance that you are most talented at – although, I'll admit that if I followed that rule I'd never run a marathon.

7) Don't overtrain. This is a pretty simple one – of course it's sometimes hard to tell when you've crossed the line. Marathon training is so difficult that simply being tired might not be a sign to ease up your training. On the other hand, you can't ignore what your body is telling you. If your pace is way off in workouts or you're getting sick constantly you should probably back off.

8) Train the mind. People probably don't appreciate the importance of training your mind to overcome pain as much as they should. Many runners who don't start until they are adults train at the same pace that they race. Of course, part of that is they are not necessarily competing – but another part of it is that their minds are not used to pushing their bodies as hard as someone who has been competing since they were a kid.

9) Rest before the race. As I've written previously, the taper is very important. Noakes states that no other running writer seems to have said anyting about tapering before Newton. In fact, many would run time trials just days before big competitions.

THURSDAY, OCTOBER 30, 2008
QUOTE – RUNNING AND SANITY

"If any psychologist will take the trouble to trace out the history of each of our prominent pedestrians he will discover that a very large proportion of them have been subject to some form of madness." – Sir Adolphe Abrahams (1961)

For those of you who don't know – "pedestrians" are what long distance runners were called back in the day. Abrahms was a doctor for the British Olympic team for several decades. So, he knew what he was talking about.

On the "Team That's What She Said" (TWSS) blog (the group I run with) someone posted a New York Times story that made training for a marathon look like more of a challenge for co-workers and spouses than for the runner. Now, they did manage to find some especially crazy runner, who I don't think qualify as the "typical" runner. One guy seemed to think it was more important to buy a $900 gadget to help him recover from long runs than to keep his family on a budget. The same guy also took his finishing medal to work the week after the race to show his already annoyed co-workers. A female runner used her commute as her training run and then didn't shower for work.

So, are runners crazier than the average person? If so, is it because crazy people are attracted to running or is it because running develops a slightly eccentric perspective – or both? Most of the comments on the TWSS blog denied that runners were more self-centered, selfish, or crazy than the general public. Most people think that the crazy people the Times found were that way before they were runners and would have been the same way regardless of whether they ever took up running. Another point made on the blog was that runners are just like any person who is obsessive about a sport or hobby. That's possible – but I'm not sure it's healthy to be obsessed about anything.

Here is what I think based on my own experiences. Generally, I feel much better psychologically when I'm training for something. Part of it is probably endorphins, part pride in accomplishing something unique, part of it is setting aside a part of my day for myself, part of it is the social connection through running (they might be crazy, but they're my kind of crazy), and part of it is just the positive feeling of being in shape.

However, there are traps that I fall into – sometimes my pride or competitiveness turn me into a bit of a jerk. Many times I expect family and friends to modify their schedules to fit my training. Luckily my wife seems to understand that it's important to me and so she doesn't take offense – but that doesn't mean it's a reasonable expectation. I can be very irritable and cranky before a big race – and sometimes afterwards if things don't go well.

That being said – all in all – I think running is a very positive thing in my life. But I know that balance is important. That's why I was a little ambivalent about starting this blog. I'm a little afraid that it's the "dark" side of running (and myself) that's leading me to write it. So far, it's been fun and helped me to focus on what I want to do this winter – so until I feel something different – I'll keep it up.

FRIDAY, OCTOBER 31, 2008
WHEN YA GOTTA GO

As part of its series of articles leading up to the NYC marathon that discuss all things tangential to the actual race, emphasizing the odd customs and traditions of marathoners, the New York Times has published an article today on porta johns. Of course the main purpose of this article is to provide an opportunity to a NYT reporter to draw upon his ability to bring poetry to any topic - such as "Their mismatched colors create a snaking kaleidoscope through the parking lots and roadways of leafy Fort Wadsworth." It also provides an opportunity to remind readers that not only do these marathoners run themselves until they almost collapse – but they are so focused on this challenge that normal rules of polite society in regards to relieving ones self in public are through the window (or pissed off the bridge – depending on the prevailing winds).

For most experienced runners it's a tradition. My college coach used to call it "shaking the dew off the lilly pad." My friend and high school teammate Todd had a nervous bladder. There were several times where he would be MIA minutes before a big race. The closest he came to missing a race was an indoor meet at Eastern Michigan our senior year. Todd had won three individual state championships by that time. The starter (the guy with the gun) was Kermit Ambrose, a legend in Michigan high school coaching – the meet was actually named after him. By the time we were in high school Kermit was 90+ and didn't seem to care much what people thought. He called Todd's name to line up – I nervously told him that Todd was still in the bathroom and that I'd check on him. Annoyed, he said, "tell him that if he shakes it more than twice he's doing something else."

At big races like NYC there is a certain strategy involved to finding the shortest porta potty lines. Runners are surprisingly lazy. Sometimes you just need to venture out a few block to find a public restroom that is shockingly vacant - even at a big race. You also need to know the lay of the land – usually there is a clump of trees/bushes where you might be somewhat "exposed" – but people usually look the other way.

As we were waiting for our friends to pass by at the Marine Corps marathon last weekend we witnessed a woman using the bushes method. The weird thing was that there was a row of unoccupied porta john's just on the other side of the road. Apparently some people just prefer nature.

The article brought up an instance where Paula Radcliffe popped a squat right to the side of the course en route to a victory in London. The article calls it "the most memorable moment in that race's history." I hope the author wasn't serious, but then again, it isn't all that often that you get to see someone drop their pants on live TV without paying for it.

SUNDAY, NOVEMBER 2, 2008
PHASE ONE: WEEK 1 OF 5

Good job to Jake and Ryan on the NYC marathon today. Jake ran a very even paced race off of a great summer of training. I'm guessing Ryan was a little disappointed – but the good news is that I'm sure he can drop a bunch of time with a little more marathon centered training. The guy has raced 20+ times this year – partied like an animal the last few weeks – organizes our crazy group – and hasn't had a real long run in months. It was a tough day – but there's no reason he can't come back with a qualifying time for Boston in the next few months.

UPDATE: The Boston qualifier is actually 59 seconds slower than I thought. So Ryan made it in by the skin of his teeth (eight seconds). I can't imagine how hard those last few miles were.

Big news from back in my home state of Michigan. My high school team took the state XC title on Saturday. My old coach, Don Sleeman is still the head coach at 70 years old. When I was a freshman he was still running sub 16 minute 5k's – not sure if that says more about my age or his. My senior year was his last state championship. We were state champs my junior and senior year – one of those years we were ranked #3 in the country. I was fifth man on my senior year and got 17th in the state. It was a pretty cool thing to be a part of and taught me that with a lot of commitment and a little talent you can accomplish a lot – especially if you are surrounded with good people.

THURSDAY, NOVEMBER 6, 2008
WHAT'S SO SPECIAL ABOUT BOSTON?

As most people know – the Boston marathon is the oldest annual marathon in the world. It was first run in 1897 – one year after the inaugural Olympics. Given the popularity of marathons these days, you might be surprised to know that of the four other "major" marathons (New York, Berlin, London, & Chicago) New York started the earliest – in 1970. Before the running boom of the 1970's marathoning was not very popular. Boston survived based on tradition.

To get more of an idea how a non-runner Bostonian view the marathon the "idiot's guide to the Boston Marathon" by ESPN's The Sports Guy is pretty good. It's not my favorite column of his (he's a great writer) – but there are some good lines like – "Any athletic activity that causes you to pee on yourself, justify it and have the justification actually make sense is something I don't want to be doing under any circumstances."

Basically he says that the Boston Marathon is an event (~500,000 people spectate) because folks get the day off from work (Patriots Day), it give people an excuse to be outside when the weather is finally getting good, get drunk, and make fun of other people. Four things that Bostonians love to do apparently.

SATURDAY, NOVEMBER 8, 2008
GREATEST RUNNING RELATED MOVIE OF ALL-TIME

There are some decent non-fiction films that show the running spirit out there – "The Billy Mills Story", "Endurance" and less effective (in my opinion) the Pre movies. But the greatest movie about running of all-time is "The Jericho Mile." I don't expect the younger generation to know "The Jericho Mile." It was a made-for-TV movie made only two years after I was born – but someone on my high school team discovered it and the movie became a ritual on nights before a big race.

The story is about Rain Murphy (played by Peter Strauss) – a man in prison for a murder that , although brutal, is forgivable (I don't want to give anything away – so I'll leave it at that). He's put in a large California prison with the worst of the worst. The prisoners are split up according to race – with Brian Dennehy playing the evil white leader. The director was Michael Mann – executive producer of Miami Vice, director of "Ali" etc.

Anyways – Rain uses running as his escape from the crushing reality of prison life. The prison "sports reporter" realizes that he's actually really good. They try to set up some real training and possibly get him to the Olympic trials.

Do yourself a favor and find the final scene on youtube. It is the greatest scene dedicated to running in the history of cinema. It doesn't really give away any of the plot – but it does give you an idea of how dated the movie is – which is of course part of the fun.

The first scene is also available on youtube. The greatest part of the first scene is when Rain's buddy yells "Kick! Kick! Kick!" If I yell that to any of my former teammates they would immediately know what I was talking about. The black guys call Rain "Lickety Split." When I was in college a random guy in Chicago called me that – it may have been the greatest day of my life (other than the day I got married of course ☺) ;).

TUESDAY, NOVEMBER 11, 2008
SCIENCE OF THE EASY RUN

Some people tend to discount the easy run as "junk mileage." Is it just about having a big number at the end of the week? Or do those easy days actually contribute to our ability to run fast?

By my count >70% of my training days before Boston will be "easy." So I hope it's important, otherwise I'm wasting a lot of time. So how specifically will these miles make me faster on April 20th?

Here are some specific physiological improvements that are made during easy runs.

Stroke Volume: The heart is really just a pump sending oxygen and other nutrients carried by the blood to organs and systems that need those nutrients to function. Stroke volume is the amount of blood that is pumped with every beat of the heart. Higher stroke volume means that the heart doesn't need to beat as quickly – and studies have shown that stroke volume is improved due to time spent running/exercising rather than intensity of training (Daniels, 2005). So even if you were to train harder – you wouldn't necessarily increase your stroke volume.

Muscle development: Easy runs increase the "number, size and distribution of the mitochondria" (Daniels, 2005). Mitochondria are the "only part of your muscle fibers in which energy can be produced aerobically" (Pfitzinger & Douglas, 2001) – they are basically little energy plants that use oxygen to produce energy for the cells they inhabit. Since 99% of energy is produced aerobically in a marathon it's important to have a lot of these little buggers. Exercise also increase the rate at which oxygen can be processed. And third, there is an increase in blood vessels in the muscle – basically improving the distribution of oxygen to all parts of the muscle. Finally muscles get better at conserving glycogen, using fat for energy, and dealing with lactic acid through easy runs (Daniels, 2005).

Running economy: Although there are many ways to increase running economy, some researchers believe that the most important factor for improved running economy (both biomechanics and cellular economy) is by the amount of accumulated miles rather than the types of workouts that you do (Pfitzinger & Douglas, 2001).

There are certainly other components that are important for marathon performance that require more intense training (lactate threshold, overall speed, & VO2 max) – but we'll get to them later. For now, all I want or need are some nice easy runs (except when our Monday group run in Fed Hill gets out of control of course).

THURSDAY, NOVEMBER 13, 2008
OLD MAN DISCUSSES HIS FAVORITE WEBSITES ABOUT RUNNING

I'm old school or maybe just old. I didn't have an e-mail address until I was in college (and even then I don't think I used it much), I didn't get a cell phone until I was a year into grad school, I remember playing "pong" and even thinking it was cool. My first video game system was an Atari 2400 – it was brand new. We didn't have a computer at home until I was in middle school. When I think how completely dependent I am on technology that has been developed since I was 18 – it's a little horrifying.

I click on Letsrun.com if I want to see what's going on in the running world or just see where "flagpole willy" thinks I should invest my money. I use marathonguide.com for the easy to use pace calculator. I use Washington running report for local running calendar and results. I head over to the USATF running routes if I'm in a new city and want to see where the locals run or if I want to measure out a new route. Of course I go to my group's page (TWSS) to find out the local workout or see what the latest post is from a growing list of bloggers like myself. Of course I keep all of this surfing to non-work hours only.

One website that's kind of cool and was started by the local running store in my hometown is half2run. It challenges people to run half marathons in half the states. They have a pretty good list of half marathons from all over the country – and a place to keep track of where you've run.

I probably look at Letsrun.com more than anything. The front page has a pretty good list of world-wide results with commentary from the sites founders wejo and rojo (the Johnson brothers).

Lost like diamonds in a haystack are some pretty good posts from the message board (even though Brian Sell once famously said of the Letsrun message board, "If I wanted to know the opinion of a 18:30 5k runner, I'd ask my wife"). Anything by Renato Canova (Italian coach to many Kenyans), Hadd, or John Kellogg are my favorites. Jack Daniels will sometimes post as "jtupper" and all runners should know about the "summer of malmo." Finally, there are plenty of characters such as the aforementioned flagpole willy, the 4:30 miler, meyerhoff, etc.

Instead of post-modern – they should call our age "post boredom."

SUNDAY, NOVEMBER 16, 2008
PHASE ONE: WEEK 3 OF 5

Running while traveling is one of my favorite things. Yes, you can get lost or wander into a really bad neighborhood. However, I don't think there's a faster way to get to know a city or a place than running in it. The plan was to run in the Smokies on Friday, but a delayed plane messed that up. Fortunately I found a pretty cool trail just a little ways off of I-85 on my way to Charlotte from ATL. It was a surreal scene of bright colored fall leaves muted by a cover of fog in the foothills of South Carolina. The last two days I've run in Atlanta – which is a cooler and funkier city than I remembered. Once you get away from the city center there are plenty of leafy residential neighborhoods to run through. The topography is slightly gentler than Baltimore – but there are plenty of hills if you look for them.

About 12 hours after I get home tonight I will get on a plane for Minneapolis. Our company headquarters is on the west side of the city – which has plenty of parks connected by a series of bike paths. Of course, the problem this time of year is the weather. It's only supposed to get down to the mid-20's this week – but there was the same forecast when I was there last November and I woke up to single digits one morning. This time I'm going to be prepared for anything.

TUESDAY, NOVEMBER 18, 2008
STAYING MOTIVATED

In the nine years since I graduated from college I've found that there are four keys to staying in good running shape.
1) Run with a group at least twice a week.
2) Find cool races to run.
3) Have goals.
4) Plan your training around these cool races and your goals.

It's pretty simple – but when I've strayed from any of these goals my motivation drops big time.

It's also important to sprinkle some less important races in your training for the "big race."

For instance – this is my schedule for races up until Boston.

1/25 – very tentatively the Miami half-marathon. Either way I'm planning on running 12-13 miles that day at marathon pace.

2/7 – USATF XC championship – with it being in Maryland this year there is really no excuse.

2/21 – Club Challenge 10 miler – I'm planning on treating this as a workout – but I MUST beat my time from last year.

3/21 – National Half-marathon in DC – This will be my main tune-up for Boston. My time here will give me a good idea of what I should shoot for on 4/20.

4/4 – I haven't found a race yet – but I need to run 15 miles at marathon pace that weekend. Let me know if anybody has any suggestions.

Longer term plans: I've decided I don't want to run a marathon more often than every 18 months – with goal races every six months.

Fall of 2009 I'm looking at maybe the Twin Cities 10 miler – which is the same day as the Twin Cities Marathon.

Past that point – who knows. But I would like to run a few marathons in Europe (Berlin, London, Paris, Rome, Rotterdam). I haven't completely ruled out an ultra – but I don't think it's my thing. My zone seems to be from 5k to half-marathon – with 10k-10 mile being my sweet spot. I would probably be happier and more comfortable just running those shorter races – but running isn't about being comfortable – it's about being comfortable about being uncomfortable.

FRIDAY, NOVEMBER 21, 2008
IT'S ALWAYS BRIGHTEST BEFORE THE DUSK: INJURIES

I've been pretty lucky with injuries during my time as a runner. But I've had a few experiences like yesterday – I was walking down the hallway when suddenly there was a sharp pain in my knee. I didn't fall or twist my knee – I was walking straight ahead and all of a sudden it felt like someone had stuck a knife in my knee. The first thought is that it's just some weird thing that will go away after a few paces. But when I got up from my cube it was still there – when I got out of the rental car it was still there – and when I slowly made my way onto the plane it was still there. I'm now sitting in the airplane. I know it might disappear after 2.5 hours of sitting down or it might be worse. (Update: it's still here) This type of pain is kind of like feeling the first rumbles of an earthquake. You start thinking – is this going to be "The One"?

Most running injuries are just from overuse – we don't know when to stop. Something must be in the water this week. My friend Ryan finally had to call it quits for awhile after he noticed a "bone protruding" from his ankle – probably caused by pushing his body too hard in the NYC marathon followed by a XC race a few weeks later – not to mention the 30 races he's run this year. Gold medal winner Kenenisa Bekele apparently ran with a possible stress fracture in a race this last week which caused him to run a "pedestrian" 15:46 for the last 5k of his race.

There are also those injuries caused by non-running accidents that have kept Olympians off their feet as well. Paul McMullen famously severed his own toe while mowing the lawn. I fell off a rented scooter in Italy a month before I was going to run the Frankfurt Marathon. I messed up my knee so bad that 80% of my training was on a stationary bike leading up to the marathon.

My worst injury was my sophomore year in high school – I was cruising through a great XC season when I started having knee problems shortly before the state meet. I basically limped through the state meet and then was on crutches for six weeks after learning I had Osgood Schlatter – an overuse injury that affects the growth plate in the knee.

Most injuries aren't so dramatic. The last two summers I've had issues that haven't forced me to stop running – but they've made it much less enjoyable. Summer of 2007 I had a problem with "runner's knee" and last summer I had plantar fasciitis for the first time in my life.

Over the next few months I'm going to write some posts about what the experts have to say about dealing with injuries and preventing them. If anybody has some interesting injury stories let me know. Injuries are part of the sport – even after I listed my injuries above I still feel like I've been lucky.

SUNDAY, NOVEMBER 23, 2008
PHASE ONE: WEEK 4 OF 5

Another big week for our Baltimore running group with several people running the Philadelphia marathon and Alyssa getting an awesome 3rd place female at the JFK 50 miler. Will had a great premier marathon at just over 2:30. The results don't seem to be up yet, so I'm not sure how everybody else did – but just getting to the start line was an act of bravery with temps below freezing this morning. This week felt more like Christmas weather than pre-Thanksgiving. I guess we're in for a long winter.

This weather is making me think about how many miserable cold weather miles I'm going to put in before April 20th. To top it off I just found out that I'll probably be in Minnesota for work the 3rd week in February, which just happens to be my biggest mileage before Boston at 100 miles for the week. I'll be lucky if the high is above 0 in Minneapolis that time of year.

The mysterious knee pain disappeared and the long run went pretty well last week – so I'm happy. Even though this next week will be almost a 20% increase in mileage and my first run over two hours in nine weeks – I'm not too worried about it. Happy Thanksgiving everybody!

SUNDAY, NOVEMBER 30, 2008
PHASE ONE: WEEK 5 OF 5

Today is like a lot of days will be in the next 20 weeks. If I had any sense I'd just put on my robe, put on some tea, and listen to some Johnny Hartman & John Coltrane with Kendra. Instead I tried to find some clothes that would protect me from the temps in the high 30's and rain. At least it wasn't windy.

The best protection against nasty weather that I've found is a feeling of superiority and a contempt for the weakness of others. In college, when we'd be running along the Chicago lakefront in January with temps below zero and hurricane force winds we'd pump our fists at the high-rise condos in fury – yelling "where are all you %#$% who clogged the running paths in July now?!!" Not that anyone could hear us, but it somehow made us feel a little less miserable.

TUESDAY, DECEMBER 2, 2008
LACTATE THRESHOLD: WHAT DOES IT MEAN? DOES IT EVEN EXIST?

Very early on in most runners' careers they hear how the build-up of lactic acid causes them to run slower and feel sore. Well, it turns out that lactic acid isn't produced in exercise and that lactate, which is produced during exercise, doesn't cause any pain or soreness in our muscles (Noakes). In fact, lactate might be a good thing for us – we just don't know. That should show you how insanely complex our bodies are when you consider that in 2008 we don't entirely understand what happens when we propel ourselves forward.

However, both Daniels and Pfitzinger talk about lactate threshold as if it still means something. Why? Well, for one we seem to be able to predict race times most reliably based on the pace at which lactate start accumulating more rapidly in the blood. Lactate accumulation is correlated with the build-up of hydrogen ions which lower pH (acidosis). Hydorgen ions can also block the uptake of calcium – which restricts muscle contraction.

So what does this all mean? Running around the "lactate threshold" (LT) point (usually 75-80% of VO2 max or 15k-20k race pace) does seem to improve running ability. And runners with lactate thresholds at a higher percentage of VO2 max race faster. The most popular LT workout is to run at LT pace for 20-40 minutes. Another LT workout is to run mile repeats at LT pace with 1-2 minutes rest.

So, a week from today when I run my first LT workout – I'll try to not confuse myself with the details and just run controlled and strong – because that's what I want to do on 4/20.

THURSDAY, DECEMBER 4, 2008
QUOTE OF THE DAY

"Hopes and dreams are just hopes and dreams until you learn how to achieve them and grant yourself permission to aggressively implement what you've learned." – Marshall Burt

QUOTE FOR THE DAY #2

I started volunteering one-on-one at a literacy center today – which made me think of an inspirational quote that means a lot to me. It's from Pema Chodron – a Shambala Buddhist nun who has written some great books on being fully awake and living a compassionate life. This is one of those quotes that you need to read several times – and try to think of how it applies to your own life before it rings true.

"We already have everything we need. There is no need for self-improvement. All these trips we lay on ourselves – the heavy-duty fearing that we're bad and hoping that we're good, the identities that we so dearly cling to, the rage, the jealousy and the addiction of all kinds never touch our basic wealth. They are like clouds that temporarily block the sun. But all the time our warmth and brilliance are right here. This is who we really are. We are one blink of an eye from being fully awake."

First, I think there is a lot to the idea that we are all Dorothy, wearing red shoes that can always get us home. That doesn't mean that we don't need to take some long trips to discover that fact – but we already have everything we need within us right now. Also, I like the idea that we don't only cling to good feelings about ourselves – but that many times we cling even more feverishly to negative feelings about ourselves – because it somehow feels "comfortable."

We grow used to putting ourselves down in some way – and it's easier to maintain that view than to look at ourselves in a more positive way. Addictions aren't just to drugs – but more often to feelings. And finally that all this negativity that we surround ourselves with is impermanent. It is as permeable as clouds – only the light of the sun is permanent and we only have to let the clouds dissipate to experience the light that we all have within ourselves.

What does this have to do with running? Everything and nothing.

SUNDAY, DECEMBER 7, 2008
PHASE TWO: WEEK 1 OF 5

It's that time of year to put some logs on the fire.

The last few weeks I've averaged 54 miles per week – the next five weeks I'm planning to average 77.5 miles per week. Plus I'll be adding a lactate threshold workout and a hills workout each week. So it will be a relatively major change to what my body has been handling lately. The basic structure of the next five weeks will be four relatively difficult days (LT workout, 90+ min run, Hills, 2+ hour run) and three recovery days (6-8 miles). My next day off will be January 8th. The good news is that my legs feel pretty lively and other than the normal aches and pains I'm pretty healthy.

This is a good time to look at the overall structure of my plan for the next 19 weeks leading up to Boston. The next 15 weeks will be split into three 5-week cycles – 4 weeks of building mileage and/or intensity and one week of "recovery." The next cycle, starting on January 12th, I plan on averaging 86.5 miles per week adding some marathon paced runs and higher intensity LT runs. The last intense cycle, starting on February 16th, I'll run 90 miles per week with a tune-up half marathon at the end of that cycle. The last four-week cycle will include LT, marathon pace training and strides – with a significant taper the last two weeks.

Endurance: Blog of a Distance Runner and Triathlete

TUESDAY, DECEMBER 9, 2008
LT WORKOUT, FIRST DOUBLE, AND SIX WORDS YOU DON'T WANT TO HEAR ON A RUN ALONE, AT NIGHT, IN BALTIMORE

I'm not going to detail every hard workout between now and Boston – but I'll probably write at least one post on every type of run. I'll cover how the experts suggest approaching it and how it worked out for me.

As I wrote in a post last week – lactate threshold is somewhat of a misnomer, but I'm going to use it for these kinds of workouts because everybody else does. Regardless of what you call it, the point of these runs is to increase the percent of VO2 max, and more importantly, the pace at which bad stuff like acidosis and reduced muscle contraction take place. To do this most experts suggest running at 15k to half-marathon pace for 20-40 minutes. You can also do LT repeats (usually 1-2 miles) with short rest.

Daniels has a more exact way of determining LT pace by what he calls your V-DOT score (I'll get into that in another post). Using Daniels method and what I thought I was capable of currently running for a half-marathon, I thought 5:35 pace would be about right. But you want to do LT runs more on feel than anything – it should be "comfortably hard" and you shouldn't have much muscle soreness during or after. You're not looking to smash the wall with a sledge hammer, but rather use the Andy Dufrain (of Shawshenk Redemption) principle of "pressure and time."

Luckily I was able to find some other members of our running group who didn't mind running a difficult workout at 7am this morning. Arjun, Brennan, Zero, and Eileen showed up on time and ready to go – unfortunately, I didn't leave myself enough time – so I was late. They were about a quarter mile into the run when we passed each other. So I ran it alone – which wasn't really that bad. I may have run a little too fast in sections and too slow in others – but I ended up at 22:30 (~5:37 pace). So, not so bad.

Today was also my first double in awhile. I try to limit doubles – but when you get around 70 miles a week it's hard to avoid them. I prefer to run doubles on days when I have a hard run – it helps to warm up the muscles and give you a chance to run less miles on recovery days. Although I usually run easy in the morning and hard in the evening – today we did the opposite so that we had daylight. I'm not going to kid you – it was tough getting out the door tonight. But after about 10 minutes I felt a little less of the aches and pains. I think that it will help me recover from this morning.

As I was trying to pry myself off the couch I made a choice about which four mile route to take. My "usual" four mile route goes north-west through the Mt. Vernon neighborhood to Bolton Hill to Reservoir Hill (between North Ave. and Druid Hill Park) and back. I had never run this route at night – and Reservoir Hill is a little sketchy – but I had run part of my other usual four miler in the morning. I like as much variety as possible on my runs. Plus – I reasoned that I have run on Monument Ave between Johns Hopkins Hospital and the JFX expressway at night, which has a bad reputation, and never had any problems. Well, the difference is that Monument is very well traveled, exposed, and you see cops pretty frequently.

About two blocks north of North Ave. on Park Ave. I passed some kids who were on the other side of the street. There was some commotion – I didn't really pay attention until I heard a kid clearly say "shoot the dumbass in the back." He could have been talking about some other dumbass – but I was the only dumbass in their immediate vicinity. Going to college in Chicago, I feel like I have some street smarts (although obviously not enough to stay out of this neighborhood at night) which told me I should just keep looking ahead and run at the same pace. Look back and they might think you're confronting them – run away fast and they might think you have a reason to run. The point is to communicate "I'm just a guy going about my business – I'm not going to cause any trouble – and I certainly don't have anything on me that would make bothering me worth it." They most definitely could have just been trying to scare me – but I'm guessing that they were doing something illegal, didn't want to get caught – so one of the kids said something they thought would scare me off. It worked.

FRIDAY, DECEMBER 12, 2008
HILLS

Hill workouts mean different things to different people. Pfitzinger writes about them in his section about resistance/weight training. He views hills as a way to strengthen the legs without using weights. Daniels agrees with this view to a point – but he also views hills as a rep workout in that it can greatly increase your heart rate over a shorter distance/slower speed than on a track.

For most people who have been on XC/track teams hills mean pain. Usually the name of the street where your coach had you do hill workouts can bring a chill to the spine many years later. At my high school, we had "5th street." Our coach marked out 400 meter and 800 meter "options." University of Michigan's team has Harvard Street – which is shorter, but steeper. At Loyola Chicago, we were forced to go to a sledding hill in Evanston that had once been a dump. It was short – so we did a LOT of them.

The worst thing about hill workouts is the last 25 meters when it feels like you're standing still, and yet your legs are burning and you feel like you might hyperventilate. But they make you stronger.

In preparation for Boston I'm going to do hills on most weeks when I have just one other "hard" workout. I may even do some downhill training as I've heard that the Boston downhills are more challenging on dead legs than you might think. This morning was my first hill workout in Druid Hill Park. I tried to take it a little easy on myself – but I still got a good burn going.

SUNDAY, DECEMBER 14, 2008
PHASE TWO: WEEK 2 OF 5

Way back in one of the first posts in this blog I said how important it was going to be to have a decent base and rest leading up to this last week. Well, I stayed on track and therefore my body handled the higher mileage and greater intensity pretty well this week. The long run was my hardest day – but my legs actually felt decent on the run today. I'm headed to yoga tonight to push out all those toxins my body has been collecting all week. Next week, I'll probably have my first track session – but otherwise it will be pretty much a copy of last week.

TUESDAY, DECEMBER 16, 2008
MY SECOND MARATHON (FRANKFURT), POST-RACE IN MILAN AND PUMPKIN BREAD RECIPE

A few weeks ago I posted some pictures of my time in Europe leading up to the Frankfurt Marathon (not in this book – but they are on the blog) in 2002. I did actually do some training in the last month – but it was mostly on a stationary bike because I messed up my knee falling off a motor scooter in Italy. I had put in quite a bit of training that summer and it was the same year as my first marathon in LA. So I had some "hay in the barn." However, I felt some fear on the starting line. For the first time in a long time I worried about whether I would finish the race.

But there were about 6-8 of my fellow exchange students who had taken the 45 minute train ride from Mannheim to watch (more support than I was used to at home) – so the pressure was on to not completely embarrass myself. The weather was on my side – it was in the 50's and about mid-way through the race – it started to gently rain. The course was pancake flat. As the miles started to flow by, my knee didn't hurt, I started to pass people and gain confidence. I did look at my watch, but I was much more focused on how my body felt, my breathing, and going after runners in front of me. The result? A better than six minute PR which still stands today.

The next day we got on a plane for Milan. Most of my friends were Norwegian and their Rosenberg team was playing Inter Milano in a Champions League game. They all had a good laugh as I had to walk downstairs backwards because of muscle soreness from the race. But it was worth it to see one of the great stadiums in European football. I knew that European soccer fans were rabid – but I didn't quite understand how rabid until I arrived in the visitors section at San Siro.

All of the fans of the visiting team were forced to sit behind one of the goals. At the corners of the stadium were 20 foot high fences separating us from the Inter fans. After Inter's first goal (luckily for us they scored a lot that day) I saw what looked like small fires breaking out in the stadium. Apparently the fans wave road flares in celebration. Also, as the game went on, there was a growing presence of police dressed in riot gear in our section. I was ready to get out of there when the game ended. But they forced us to stay in our seats for 30 minutes until the entire stadium was empty. They walked us back to the buses and we got a police escort back to our hotel. Yankees vs. Red Sox ain't nothin'.

As a reward for all those who read through my ramblings I have written out my family's recipe for pumpkin bread – which was a success at Arjun, Melissa, and Brennan's Thanksgiving on Saturday.

3 cups white granulated sugar
4 eggs
2/3 cups water
3 1/3 cups flour
1 cup cooking oil
2 cups pumpkin
1 tsp. cinnamon
1 ½ tsp. salt
1 tsp. nutmeg
2 tsp. baking soda
1 tsp. vanilla

Mix as you're adding ingredients. You'll need a fairly large mixing bowl.

Grease baking pans heavily. Makes enough for two loaves. Fill each pan about half-way. Bake at 350 degrees for 45-60 minutes until cooked through the center (use toothpicks to test for "doneness").

Enjoy!

FRIDAY, DECEMBER 19, 2008
CLARENCE DEMAR – "MR DE MARATHON"

I might be wrong – but I'm guessing that no one reading this blog has heard of "Mr. de Marathon" before. The only reason I know anything about him is that he is in Noakes' book "Lore of Running." He won the Boston marathon a record seven times and ran it 33 times – the last time at the age of 65. Some of the years he won had some soft times, but he ran a 2:18 in 1922 – no easy jog. DeMar only won the Boston marathon once during the ages of 22-33 because he had been told he had a heart problem and that as a strict Baptist he believed the desire for "selfish victory" was immoral. So – maybe there is some hope for us "old men."

The one quote I found from him was "Run like hell and get the agony over with."

His training doesn't seem to have consisted of much quality work – it was mostly 100 mile weeks with 20 mile runs as his main run for the week. Speed work mostly came from 10 mile races.

MONDAY, DECEMBER 22, 2008
QUOTE OF THE DAY

One of my favorite books is "River Horse", by William Least Heat-Moon. The book recounts the author's trip from New York City to the mouth of the Columbia River at the Pacific Ocean. He made the trip by boat – with only a few dozen miles of portage. He traveled the rivers, lakes, and canals of America – which give him plenty of time to write about history, geography, and ecology of our country. I think what interests me most about the book is how a voyage like this is a very strong metaphor for life – especially a voyage on such a flowing and ever-changing thing as a river.

This quote is from a part of the book where he is on the Missouri River in South Dakota.

"I thought how far I was from where and when this journey began, how I was so distant from that fellow passing for me twenty months ago, the one so eager to learn the secrets of river passage. Could he – the me of that moment – and I sit down together, he would want to know that I knew and absorb what I had experienced, and he would regard me enviously, just as I do those men who have returned from the moon. But there would be forever a difference between him and me: I went and he did not. He set the voyage in motion, but he could not take it. Just as I, who lay on the Dakota hill, could not know whether his boat Nikawa would reach the Pacific, he could never see the outcome of his preparations, unless somewhere, on some far other side, time permits us to meet our past selves, all those we have been. Our physical components change every seven years, so our brains are continuously passing along memories to a stranger; who we have been is only a ghostly fellow traveler. As for me, what might I learn from him who laid out the voyage or from all those other I once was .
. .
What a report I might deliver to them about where they have sent me! And

how they could remind me of first kisses and death, the Haitian mountains at sunset and Ozark hills at night. They could redraw the faded lines of the long map of my journey here, point out clearly where it was I took a road other than the one they intended, and they could tell me whether they liked that divagation or not, whether they found it a good one or rankly stupid. Were human memory total and perfect, perhaps I'd be only one person from start to finish, but forgetfulness cuts me off from who I've been so that hourly I am reborn. To twist Santyana's words, I who cannot fully remember my past am condemned to proceed without it."

The last sentence seems to say that our imperfect memory is somehow a limitation – but he's really saying that the fading of memories allow us to change – which is not only positive, but it's necessary if we are to adapt and thrive in a world that is ever-changing.

To outsiders it might seem that running is about routine and familiarity. But for me, running is addictive because it's about transformation. Whether it's a six-month marathon training cycle or an easy four miler – I run because I expect that the experience will change me – if not from who I am, than from who I might become. Thankfully, the painful memories of past marathons are only good enough to help me to change my methods – but not so perfect to stop me from doing another one.

WEDNESDAY, DECEMBER 24, 2008
HURTIN'

I don't want this blog to be a constant stream of whining and complaining. But I think it is worthwhile to note when I've reached a red line and how my body is reacting to training now vs a few months from now. I had a hard time getting in my easy four miler last night and an even harder time with my medium long run this morning. My legs aren't completely trashed – but they're feeling "dead." My whole body feels fatigued and I just feel "out of it."

I think it's from a combination of factors. This will be my first week over 80 miles in awhile. I notice that I can recover pretty well at about 75 miles per week – anything more than that and my body seems to protest. Also – I ran my tempo run yesterday a little too fast – especially because it was only a few days after a 19 mile run. Tomorrow will be easy – but Friday I'm planning to do a hill workout in Ann Arbor with my old running group and a long run on Saturday. I don't know how in shape they all are – but I'm sure someone will push the pace.

Although next week will be another high-mileage week – I will get three easy days in a row on Sunday, Monday, & Tuesday. Plus I'm hoping that a few days of warmth in FLA will make running outside feel like not such a chore.

The number one thing I need to do is focus on recovery activities – including elevating my legs and cold whirlpools. And of course nutrition – but realistically that probably won't get better until after the holidays.

FRIDAY, DECEMBER 26, 2008
THE SEVEN DEADLY SINS AND RUNNING

As I was questioning why I was leaving my warm bed this morning at 6:20am for the icy roads of Ann Arbor, I decided to snap a picture of my parents' street to put on the blog. As soon as I had taken the shot the answer came; pride. I have to admit that's a major reason why I put myself through what many people would describe as torture. Although I wasn't raised Catholic, like my wife, I did have a fare amount of German Lutheran guilt as a child. I decided to think about what other of the seven deadly sins might be important factors in motivating me to run.

Sloth – This might seem the antithesis of most type-A runners. But I think that a certain sloth like personality when you're away from running is important. If you have the go-go-go mentality all the time then you'll probably not get the proper rest that you need.

Envy – Come on, admit it. If you're a runner there is another runner who you envy in terms of their pure talent or work ethic or ability to recover. Although we might say "running is a competition against the clock" there is always somebody who we'd love to knock down a level because we envy what they can do.

Gluttony – For the most part I think you need to have the appetite of a rabbit to be a good runner. As Frank Shorter would say "the hungry wolf leads the pack" but from time to time it's good to be a glutton as a runner. Romans who visited vomitoriums would not be uncomfortable at the pre-race pasta meal.

Lust – As with music many people get into sports to impress members of the opposite sex. Even as a married guy, lust plays a part in motivating my running. There are enough things that I screw-up on as a husband – that it's good to have something that Kendra thinks is impressive about me. Like power – doing something well can be a great aphrodisiac.

Greed – For most runners this doesn't apply directly to money – but rather place. Wanting first place all for one's self might be thought as a type of greed – for some it is the most important sin to have in terms of being a good runner.

Wrath – This is probably the least connected to running – but I guess it can be thought of as a certain form of the competitive mind set. This is probably related to greed and envy – as it's usually better runners who regularly beat me for who I reserve my wrath.

TUESDAY, DECEMBER 30, 2008
QUOTE OF THE DAY

"If at first you don't succeed, you can always become an ultramarathoner."
– Bruce Fordyce

Apologies to Alyssa – but that one was too funny to pass up. Fordyce is one of the most decorated ultra marathoners – having won the famous Comrades Marathon (90 km) eight years in a row.

It made me think about how one becomes a distance runner in general. I was cut from my middle school baseball team in 7th grade – a friend of mine convinced me to run on the track team. Baseball was my favorite sport to watch – the Detroit Tigers won the World Series when I was seven years old. At that age, it left an impression.

I played soccer throughout grade school – I think I was actually pretty good – but I wasn't into it enough to stand out. In basketball I just barely made the "A" team my 8th grad year – I also played volleyball and wrestled my 8th grade year. I was marginally good in all those sports except for wrestling – where I sucked. But in 8th grade I ended up winning the mile in the Ann Arbor city wide meet in 5:08. That success pretty much sealed what I would do in high school and college.

In college, I found that I needed to go all the way up to running 10k on the track (26 laps) before I could win anything. The odd thing about post-collegiate running is that the marathon is king – and it's not really my race. Using my 10k time from college, I should be able to run about 16 minutes faster than my PR in the marathon. Even if I had started training for the marathon right after college at 22 years old – I don't think I could have run that fast. My body just isn't made for it. So what am I doing training this hard for something that's not really "my thing"?

For one – the major marathons are incredible events. People from all walks of life want to be a part of them – people will scream their heads off for hours on end for complete strangers. It can be transformative for people who never thought of themselves as athletes and yet find the way to finish one. As a runner, I am used to racing in front of family and friends – but the New York or Boston marathons give me the chance to be a part of a major sporting event. There are 10k's or half-marathons with thousands of people – but it's not the same.

After a few more marathons I'll probably focus more on 5k's to half-marathons because that's where I could be most successful. But while I'm still at an age that I can run a decent marathon – I want to see what I can do. I'll never run a 5k or 10k faster than what I did in college – but I can easily PR in the marathon. The question is how much?

SUNDAY, JANUARY 4, 2009
PHASE TWO: WEEK 5 OF 5 - POOLSIDE

Yes, I am writing this poolside in Key West. Blogging may have been light this week, but I got in some good running. Today I ran two "laps" of Key West for a 21 mile run. Thankfully it was cloudy and even raining a little – so I was able to run pretty quick for the last half. I probably averaged somewhere near 6:15 pace for the last 10 miles. This week my mileage comes down a bit – but I have two quality runs – a threshold workout and a VO2 max workout.

It's been nice to not need to cover every inch of my body with clothes down here. On Wednesday Kendra and I bundled-up to run the Fairfax Four Miler back in Virginia. I was planning to run it as a threshold workout – but either the course was short or I got a little excited running a race with 1800 people. I ended up running sub 21:30 pretty comfortably. They had to change the course because a power line went down on the original course – so it very well could have been short.

Next week, I need to start focusing on nutrition. The holidays and Key West have led to me gaining a little weight – even with all the miles I've been running.

WEDNESDAY, JANUARY 7, 2009
2009 GOALS

Since I'm writing a running blog I guess I'm contractually obligated to put down my goals for the upcoming year, so that I can either laugh at them next year, or feel proud of myself.

In order of priority:

1) Run 3,650 miles for the year. Basically average 10 miles per day. I think this is the most important goal because it will have the largest effect on me making my other goals. Plus it seems like the goal most under my control.
2) Sub 2:30 at Boston. The major reason for this blog is to keep myself focused through training for Boston so that I give myself a shot at a sub-2:30. I know this isn't going to be easy – but I should be able to run it – and now is as good a time as any to do it.
3) Run 52:30 for 10 miles. My goal race for the fall will probably be the Army 10 miler. This might even be tougher than the sub 2:30 – the major factor will be how well I recover from Boston.

SUNDAY, JANUARY 11, 2009
PHASE 3: WEEK 1 OF 5

The lower mileage this week certainly helped bring a little zip back to my legs. We went out to the site of the national USATF XC meet in Derwood, MD yesterday. We ran 2k and 1k repeats with 1k rest for a total of 12k. I ran the 2k's in approximately 5:30 pace per mile and the 1k's in just under 5:10 pace. Given the rolling course I felt pretty good about that. I hadn't run a XC course with spikes in over 10 years – it felt good.

Over the next four weeks, I'm planning on averaging just under 90 miles per week. I'll have three threshold runs, two VO2 workouts, a marathon pace run, two runs over 20 miles, and a 12k race. The key will be being able to recover from my workouts without sacrificing mileage. I've still got 14 weeks before Boston – so I can't burn myself out either – it's all about walking the tightrope. Hopefully better nutrition and more active recovery will help me out.

TUESDAY, JANUARY 13, 2009
VO2 MAX

VO2 max refers to the maximum amount of oxygen that can be processed by the body in a certain time period. It is expressed as liters of oxygen per minute. In other words – it is the capacity of the cardiovascular system and peripheral systems (muscle groups) to take in oxygen, deliver it to muscles, process oxygen, and deal with the by-products. VO2 max can be tested by increasing pace every minute until the runner is going all out. Expired air is collected in a bag during the test. Heart rate is taken at the end and lactate levels are measured two minutes after the end of the test – when lactate is the highest.

Along with lactate threshold and running economy – VO2 max is an important determinant to distance running. It is most important for distances up to 10k.

So how do you improve VO2 max? Interval training is the most efficient way to improve VO2 max. Usually this is done by running at 3k-5k pace (usually 95-100% of VO2 max) for 3-5 minute intervals with recovery times that are equal to, or a little less, than the time of the interval. According to Jack Daniels, the amount of total weekly interval-paced training should be up to eight percent of total mileage.

THURSDAY, JANUARY 15, 2009
THE PERILS OF WINTER RUNNING NEAR WATER & DUBAI

Compared to where I did most of my running growing up – I can't really complain about training in Baltimore in the winter. In the Midwest it isn't just the cold that's miserable – it's the footing. The constant concentration of where you are going to place your foot. Is that bump of snow so frozen hard that I'm going to turn my ankle? Is that dusting of snow hiding a patch of ice? And then, despite this level of concentration, you inevitably fall.

After several months of surviving this kind of thing – you tend to start tempting fate. In high school, we used to go down to the Huron River in Ann Arbor – where large swaths of ice would form by the banks. The middle of the river was ice free – we would kick through the ice nearest land – attempting to "free" the ice into the river. If the ice was especially thick – then one of us might go out onto the ice – trying to use our body weight to start a crack, without falling through. Although, I fell through once that I remember. Once you've survived running home four miles, soaked to the waist, in sub-freezing temperatures, it seems like there isn't anything you can't do.

In college, we ran a lot along Lake Michigan. In the winter, the waves can get surprisingly high. On one such day we ran out on a cement breaker that separated a marina from the lake. Just as we got out to the very end of the breaker – a three foot wave came from our right side. Most of the other guys had their legs taken out from under them, but were able to stay on the breaker. I was not so lucky. The wave swept me into the water. So, that time I got to run home four miles (why did I always do this so far from home?) soaked from head to toe. I can't remember exactly how cold the air temp was – but it was at least in the 20's.

Well, today I had a kind of icy déjà vu. I was running through Loyola Maryland's campus toward the "magic path." To get to the magic path I had to cross a stream. There was actually a dusting of snow up there – so I was being very careful going from rock to rock. Well, my last rock wasn't sturdy – it started moving and before I knew it I was in the stream. Luckily, only my left side and my hands got wet – but I landed hard on my hip and forearm on some rocks. There was that momentary "I want my momma" feeling – but then I knew that the best thing would be to get moving to keep hypothermia at bay. The hip is a little sore – but it didn't hurt while I was running. I even got to have a tough guy moment, when I had my wife feel how the outside of my left sleeve and left pant leg had frozen solid on the way home.

On a different note – the Dubai marathon is tonight (well, actually tomorrow, but tonight our time). It is the richest marathon in the world with a $250k first prize and $1 million dollar bonus for the world record. Geb is in it – and he sounds confident that he can break his own record. Even if he doesn't – there are a lot of talented guys in it – so it should be interesting.

SUNDAY, JANUARY 18, 2009
PHASE 3: WEEK 2 OF 5

I could feel disappointed last week from an intensity standpoint – I had some GI issues during the workout on Tuesday and Saturday I decided that 10 degrees was too cold for a time trial. But I ran 42 miles in three days at the beginning of the week without taking too much of a toll on my legs. Plus, I felt pretty good on my 20 miler today. My legs used to feel weak after running for two hours – but I felt strong through 2 hours 20 minutes today on a hilly run in Patapsco State Park.

This week will be my first week over 90 miles and in a nice treat I'll get to run my marathon pace run in Miami on Sunday. We seemed to have gotten past our worst cold snap of the year. Not that we're going to see blooming flowers any time soon – but I doubt we'll have many more days under 15 degrees.

TUESDAY, JANUARY 20, 2009
THE UNIQUE PERSPECTIVE OF THE DISTANCE RUNNER

For me running is not only about working out – it's about discovery and freedom. I sometimes imagine a map, only existing in my head, that has lines showing everywhere I've run. Of course the lines would be most heavily drawn in the places I've lived. The countless times that I ran through the Arboretum in Ann Arbor, on the lakefront in Chicago, beside Sunset Cliffs in San Diego, along the Rhine in Mannheim, and on the magic path in Baltimore. Travel favorites would include a trail in Hawaii that ended at a waterfall, a run in the Smokies where I saw a bear, a sunny day in San Francisco running up to Coit Tower, and on the Philosopher's weg across from Heidelberg.

Well, today I drew another line on that map that had as much to do with the day as the place. I had been debating whether I would go to the inauguration for a while now. I was supposed to do a hard run this morning – but the roads were still too slick. I started watching the coverage and suddenly felt like I needed to be there. The major reason that I had decided not to go was that it was going to be almost impossible to get down there. But if I could find a place to park in Rock Creek Park – just south of Silver Spring – I decided I could run the six miles down to The Mall.

Believe it or not, I-95 was pretty clear from Baltimore to DC. I made it to Silver Spring by 10:30am or so. I drove down 16th street and entered Rock Creek Park – finding a parking spot near a picnic area. There was nobody around. It was odd that just a half-dozen miles away there was one of the largest crowds this nation has ever seen. I started down the path – running along the half frozen Northwest branch of Rock Creek. After a few miles I followed a few other runners over to 16th street. I headed downhill – the people multiplying as the blocks went by. Finally at "R" street they blocked off traffic to vehicles. Eventually I passed St. Johns Church – where the prayer service that Obama family attended was held this morning. Then traffic was forced west at H street – I eventually made it to The Mall just west of the Washington Monument.

The crowds were most thick around giant TV screens. Since I was a child, The Mall has always seemed incredible to me – today it was simply magical. I thought that I probably couldn't get much closer and I wanted to see everything from a different perspective. So, I made what might seem like an odd choice. With only 15 minutes until the swearing in I decided to run over to Arlington Cemetery. I remembered the last time I was there that it was a great view of The Mall – and I figured that I could listen to the inaugural speech later. So I made my way past the Lincoln Memorial and over the Arlington Bridge. I obeyed the policeman who reminded me that there was no "jogging" in the Cemetery – and briskly walked up to the Tomb of the Unknown Soldier.

When I arrived, they were just starting the changing of the guard. I hadn't really even thought about the fact that they would still be doing the changing of the guard of the tomb at the same moment that a different changing of the guard would be occurring across the Potomac. There were about six or seven people at the Tomb. Mostly family members and servicemen I guessed. As they went through their motions I could actually hear Obama's voice from the huge speakers on the mall – as he took the oath of office. After he finished there was a huge roar of the crowd – just as the sentinels walked off the mat. It was pretty cool.

Maybe it would have been more exciting to be down on the mall with the crowd at that moment. But over a million people did that – only half a dozen saw the same thing I did. Today running wasn't about the miles (although I ran about 16) it was about allowing me to experience something that I couldn't have done any other way.

SUNDAY, JANUARY 25, 2009
PHASE 3: WEEK 3 OF 5

Witness the dedication of your intrepid blogger as he posts from the ATL airport. Dedication and the fact that I want to spend time with my understanding wife when I finally get home this evening. I've been in Miami this weekend – partly for the sun and the beach and partly for the Miami Half-marathon. The start was at 6:15am this morning. Which means that other than a short nap on the first leg of my plane trip – I've been up since 4am.

The plan was to run at marathon pace. I didn't want to go all out because I have a hundred mile week coming up and it's still too early to push my body like that. The trick is to slowly stress my body so it can best perform on 4/20 – not to kill myself with three months to go. I even backed off from using 2:30 as my "marathon pace." So I shot for a 1:16. Luckily another Falls Road team member, Brennan, had the same goal pace (there were seven of us who made the trip). We ran together for most of the race – which made it much easier.

I ended up running 1:16:18 – just above my goal pace. Which all things considered (we stayed on South Beach) was fine. Even with the early start, it was a fun race and I'd consider doing it again. The challenge is going to be the workout on Tuesday. I'm running my longest tempo workout (4X2 miles) with only one day rest from the half. I'll probably not run quite as fast as I've done my other tempo workouts – given that it will be twice the tempo mileage. Other than running 100 miles in a week for the first time since the fall of 2007 – the rest of the week shouldn't be too bad.

TUESDAY, JANUARY 27, 2009
MOVING UP TO PREMIUM

For most of the time I've been a runner my nutrition has been an afterthought. I knew it could make a different – but for whatever reason I just haven't made it a priority. Given that I have a friend in our running group who is a nutritionist (Melissa Bosslet) and that I'll need every trick in the bag to get under 2:30 at Boston – I decided to set up an appointment to get myself a plan.

Melissa works for EB Nutrition in Rockville, MD and she happens to be a great runner – which was important to me, because I wanted someone who knows what I'd need given my marathon training.

I filled in a food diary for three days before we met – and then we talked about what I thought I needed improvement on as well as my goals and amount of exercise. She determined that I would need at least 3,000 calories per day, that I needed to cut sugar, combine carbs with protein, eat smaller portions more often throughout the day, add variety, add more fish etc . . .

She gave me a list of suggested foods to eat as well as avoid – and sample meals for my week. In my first grocery visit I spent an insane amount of money – but there were a lot of staples that I won't need to buy every week. Other than a few days in Miami, I've remained true to the diet and it's already showing results. This morning I had my best tempo workout in a very long time (4X2 mi; ~11 min per) only two days after running a decent effort at the Miami Half-marathon. So, if you want to see what you can really accomplish I suggest you find someone like Melissa to help you out.

WEDNESDAY, JANUARY 28, 2009
EXCLUSIVE "INTERVIEW" WITH THE LAST AMERICAN BOSTON CHAMP: GREG MEYER

When Greg Meyer's son was in elementary school he once told a friend that his father had won the Boston Marathon. "Your dad's Kenyan?!" came the response. No, Greg Meyer isn't Kenyan – he's from that other great hotspot of distance running – the American Midwest. Specifically from Grand Rapids, MI – the same area of Michigan as current star Dathan Ritzenhein. From Grand Rapids, he went to the University of Michigan in my hometown of Ann Arbor. After several All-American seasons at Michigan he moved to Boston to work and train with the likes of Bill Rodger and Bob Hodge.

Greg worked his way into the distance ranks. When he first moved to Boston he was a clerk for Bill Rodgers' running store – before finally being sponsored by Brooks. Greg had many strong performances through the years – but it can be argued that no American runner has had a better eight months as Greg did between the end of August 1982 till the end of April 1983. I suggest everyone read his training log – which is available online – during that period. He broke the American 20k record, won the Chicago marathon, broke the American 15k record, won the 30k OHME race in Tokyo, won the Cherry Blossom 10 miler and won Boston in 2:09:00 – only six second off the record. He even went to a Willie Nelson concert that was memorable enough that he included it in his blog.

I met Greg when he worked with my mother in development at the University of Michigan. I recently told him about my blog and asked if he might grant me an "interview." He said yes, so I sent him some questions via e-mail and he responded.

BI: When did you first set your sights on winning Boston? Was it something you thought about as a kid? Or was it not really on your radar until after college?

GM: First set my sites on Boston only after moving there in '78. What pissed me off enough to run a marathon was my friend Tommy Leonard . . . of Elliot Lounge fame . . . telling me someday I could be as good as Vinny Flemming (Vinny. . .also a friend and teammate on the Greater Boston Track Club was a 2:14 guy at Boston). Getting my ass kicked my Seko and others in '81 was motivation for '83.

(Note: For more details around his motivation and how he won Boston there is a great first person account he wrote for Runners World a few years ago.)

BI: What do you think was/were the most important aspect(s) of your training for the marathon?

GM: Most important aspect of my training was running on the course multiple times a week. Coach Squires' fartlek 20 miles on the course were great as well. That and seven years of averaging 100 MPW.

BI: What was your training group like in Boston? Were the guys loose with each other? Competitive? And how did that group help/hinder your development?

GM: Training group was amazing. . . Bill Rogers (2:09), Randy Thomas (2:11), Bob Hodge (2:10), Tim Donovan (2:16) . . who thankfully was my whipping boy on some runs . . . but a great partner . . . those and others!

BI: What was your strategy going into the 1983 Boston race?

GM: Strategy was only to win . . . don't charge the up hill or down hill . . . but throw little surges to keep the pace fast. Benji changed that . . . took the pace . . . I only had to do one real surge before Heartbreak.

BI: What was the coolest thing that's happened to you as a result of winning Boston?

GM: Coolest thing since Boston . . . people still ask me about running . . . and it gives me instant credibility with the kids I coach . . . oh, and throwing out a first pitch at Fenway was VERY COOL. Even my grown kids thought so!

TUESDAY, FEBRUARY 3, 2009
BE THE CHIHUAHUA!

In honor of the National Cross-Country race this weekend in Derwood, MD – I thought I'd write a story of another important XC race in my life. It was the week of the Michigan State XC meet my junior year of High School (yes, jerks, that was a long time ago). Our team had won every meet that fall and my buddy Todd Snyder had won every individual title. But this was different, it was the state meet and we were supposed to win – the toughest kind of pressure.

Our coach, Don Sleeman had been at Ann Arbor Pioneer high school for ~25 years at this point – in fact, he's still coaching after 40 years and his team won a state championship just last year. Sleeman was a Sergeant in the Air Force before he started teaching and coaching. His main motto was "Pain purifies." Of course the guys who had come before us said that he had "softened" over the years – but he was still pretty intimidating at the time.

The first two weeks of practice in August were always hell – no one pushed their team harder. But he knew when to back off – and feeling the pressure that we were all feeling the week before the state meet he decided that we all needed some humor in our lives. After our normal stretching routine – he said he had a newspaper column to read to us. This was normal for him – there were copies of newspaper articles on running pasted all over the walls of his office. But this article was different – first of all it was about dogs – but more generally it was about how the right amount of motivation and focus we can overcome any obstacle.

The article was a column by the Chicago Tribune's Mike Royko. It was about a male Chihuahua in Florida that had been sauntering around the neighborhood, when suddenly an urge overcame him as he saw the neighborhood female Rottweiler. The urge proved much stronger than any fear that pup must have had regarding their size differential, and believe it or not he successfully impregnated the Rottweiler. As with all great American stories – we know this is not urban legend because a lawsuit was involved. The owner of the Rottweiler sued the owner of the Chihuahua. Coach Sleeman said that the most important thing for us to remember that coming Saturday was to "be the Chihuahua." Looking back, I think he might have feared that we might become the Rottweiler.

That Saturday we toed the line on a chilly Michigan November day – and in the stillness before the gun fired – one of my teammates yelled out – "BE THE CHIHUAHUA!" Of course, in the first 10 meters we almost fell over ourselves laughing – but any tension we had in our bodies was gone. We went on to win the State Championship. We won in such an impressive manner that we ended up being ranked the 3rd best cross country team in the country by USA Today.

So on Saturday, as we toe the line against the Rottweilers of Ritz, Meb, Fam and others – let's remember to be the Chihuahua!

Ryan – please don't take that literally.

SUNDAY, FEBRUARY 8, 2009
PHASE 3: WEEK 5 OF 5

Well, I ended the week a little hobbled. Running in XC spikes yesterday at Derwood made my plantar fasciitis flare up. I almost turned back in the first mile of my run today – but eventually it warmed up enough so that I could run without a limp. But I think I was still landing weird on my right foot. I probably wasn't smart to run 17 miles today – but I don't think I did any lasting damage.

It was a beautiful day on the course yesterday – very cool to see an event of that level in our backyard. Even though the weather was good the course was pretty muddy in places. My 42:13 was at least a minute off my goal – but given the conditions I'm not too disappointed.

This week will be the lowest mileage week I've had in over a month. Although the mileage will be down, including a day off with a massage, the intensity will still be there. I'm supposed to do a 4X2 mi on Tuesday (we'll see how I feel) – but the main workout will be Saturday with my first long run with tempo: 18 miles total 2 mi easy 4X1 mi T pace with 1 min rest 7 mi easy 3 mi T pace 2 mi easy. I'm going to be running this type of workout more consistently as I get closer to the marathon: running fast when my glycogen supplies are low. It will be a good test.

TUESDAY, FEBRUARY 10, 2009
BOOK REVIEW: "A RACE LIKE NO OTHER"

The book focuses on the 2007 New York Marathon – which, coincidentally I ran. The author Liz Robbins is a sportswriter for the NY Times – a newspaper that doesn't always seem to cover running very seriously. But I was pleasantly surprised with this book. There was a good balance of in-depth reporting of the top runners – along with "regular" people who were running the marathon to overcome great odds (cancer survivor/recovering alcoholic).

Also, there were some decent chapters about the history of the marathon. How the huge even that we know today went through some difficult developmental years. Some of the most interesting sections were about the people who come out to support the runners year after year. There aren't many sports where "regular" people have fans. Having experienced 1st Avenue in Manhattan – I can say that it's one of the most incredible experiences I've had as a runner.

So, if you're looking for a book to inspire you for the NYC marathon next fall – this is one to pick up.

THURSDAY, FEBRUARY 19, 2009
THE TWO "I'S"

I've been putting off writing about this subject, because I don't want to jinx myself. But I don't know any runner who hasn't had to deal with at some point. The two "I's", of course, are injuries and illness.

As I'm at the beginning of the four toughest weeks of training in my life, I have to understand what I can run through – and when I need to sacrifice some mileage to ensure that I can battle another day.

The biggest physical problem I've had is plantar fasciitis. It's the inflammation of the plantar fascia, which runs along the bottom of the foot. The pain is normally felt on the heal – kind of like stepping on a steel spike with every stride. I've spent about $80 on various treatments – but a little $4 plastic ball with bumps seems to work the best.

It's possible for the plantar to rupture – but I'm most worried about it affecting my stride – which in turn could injure something else. For instance, the day after the XC race was miserable. The plantar pain caused me to run on the outside of my right foot – which strained my upper ankle. It probably wasn't the smartest thing for me to do – but I was already under my planned mileage for that week.

My wife makes fun of me because I never get sick – but this morning I woke up with a scratchy throat. I don't like to whine – but there's always the thought that it might turn into something worse. So I decided to split up my 15 miler into a morning an evening run. But by the time the evening came around I had a bunch of work left to do and I was hungry for dinner – so I bailed. I probably could have gotten through the run – but my gut said it's time to rest.

Why did I run through a miserable run the Sunday after USATF XC and not tonight? Some of it might be the fact I drove down to DC for the run with some other guys, and tonight would have been by myself – but it's just something you have to decide – is this run going to help or hurt me?

As sane as it might seem that nobody should run through pain caused by overuse – there is no way that you can run your best without doing that from time to time. I know that some people will disagree with me – but running is about handling pain of all kinds. The key is figuring out the difference between aggravating pain and debilitating pain.

SUNDAY, FEBRUARY 22, 2009
PHASE 4: WEEK 2 OF 5

My first thought about my training this last week is that it was the most disappointing week I've had since I started my training plan for Boston. After getting sick on Thursday I had to cut my mileage short – so I ended up with 11 less miles than planned.

But, on second thought, my quality days were not too bad. On Wednesday I had my first track workout in a few months – 6X1000m – it actually went a little better than I had hoped. Every repeat got a little faster – with my last 1000m in 4:48 mile pace. And today I made it through a tough 10 mile course without embarrassing myself at the Club Championships in Columbia, MD. Most importantly, our team won the overall championship, which was not completely expected, and a lot of fun.

This week is the highest total that I have planned in my 24 weeks of marathon training. I think I'm on the backside of being sick – but I'm going to have to play it by ear. And I'm running a "marathon" this weekend. Really it's just a long distance run – but I'm sure it won't be a walk in the park.

THURSDAY, FEBRUARY 26, 2009
THE POWER OF THE GROUP

This week, baring a catastrophe, should be my highest mileage week ever (110 miles). So, what is a content, married, 31 year old doing pushing himself harder than ever before in his life? Yes, some of it can be attributed to the tick tock of the biological clock I hear in my legs. But I think the most important factor is my training group.

You might say – "I thought that distance runners are a lonely bunch – who are running away from . . . er . . . something." Not that I don't enjoy a good run by myself – but we ARE humans – social creatures at heart. And we are motivated by the same things that all people are.

The most famous post-collegiate running group in the US is Hansons from Michigan. Brian Sell, who was not exactly a star in college, used the group training method to help put him on an Olympic team. Frank Shorter, Bill Rodgers, Alberto Salazar, Robert Cheruiyot, Haile Gebrelasse – all of them had a good nucleus of people to train alongside them – and even challenge them from time to time.

But I don't envy them at all for what we have in Baltimore.

We train in freezing cold and in the sweltering heat;
We train in the city, in the woods, and on the track;
We feel good for each other's accomplishments, but
We warn each other, with a wink, "I'll get you next time";

We're not always the fastest – but as Ryan says, "nobody is more awesome."
We're the adult softball team without the beer gut;
The poetry/philosophy club without the pen or paper;

The church without a god, but we do have regular services;
And when we pass around the plate for offering it comes back with blood and pain and stories;
And that is enough for me.

SUNDAY, MARCH 1, 2009
PHASE 4: WEEK 3 OF 5

Well – I guess a celebration is in order – I ran my highest mileage week total ever this week. Best of all – my legs feel good. I ran a full marathon today – yes I know that sounds crazy – but I had a 24 miler scheduled – there was a local marathon (B&A trail) – so I though what's two extra miles? Luckily some other guys who wanted a long run came along for most of it – which made it much easier mentally.

We started out the first mile in almost exactly seven minutes. From there we gradually got faster – until we were running almost 6:30 pace at the half-way mark. Although not every mile was faster than the last – we did get to about 6:20 pace by the 19th mile. My plan was to push the last 10k – which I ended up running in 38:38 (~6:14 pace). My total time was 2:52:20 – although my chip fell off on the trail (I'm not sure how) – so I didn't get an official time. I'm happiest because my legs feel pretty good. We'll see how this week goes – but I'm feeling pretty confident right now.

This week includes a little dip in mileage – the question will be how the weather and my travel schedule at the beginning of the week will affect my mileage. We're supposed to get eight inches of snow tonight and I have to drive to NJ tomorrow for work.

THURSDAY, MARCH 5, 2009
MEDITATION & RUNNING

Before I moved to Baltimore I used to meditate fairly regularly. My uncle is an alumnus of Naropa University – a college in Boulder, CO that was started by the founder of Shambhala International, Chogyam Trungpa. One of his professors was the poet Allen Ginsburg. Anyways my uncle led a weekly meditation group in Ann Arbor which I attended pretty regularly. It was such a part of my life that my uncle officiated our wedding.

It seems most people think that meditation is about letting your mind go blank. It's actually about focusing your mind on your immediate surroundings and your body – instead of the incessant flow of thoughts through your brain about the past or the future. It's about quieting the mind – not shutting it down. The concentration should be on the breath and one's posture. This concentration on the simple task of breathing and sitting is supposed to allow you to become more open to what is actually occurring around you – to stop applying your own schemas on everything around you and just observe them for what they are without judgment.

So what does this have to do with running? Well, the last few days have been pretty intense for me from a work perspective. And yesterday was just plain tiring – it was about 15 hours from the time I left my hotel room for a run yesterday morning until I got home to Baltimore. And there was no real mental break – unless driving counts.

I started my run tonight completely distracted. I was on my own and supposed to run 8X1 mile with only 30-40 seconds rest. My first mile wasn't too bad – but my second mile was about 15 seconds slow. My mind was somewhere else. So instead of panicking, I focused on relaxing my breathing, relaxing the muscles of my face, relaxing my shoulders, driving my knees, shortening my stride, keeping my arm carriage relaxed and controlled etc . . . I've found if I keep cycling through all these in my head – it's actually enough to occupy my mind and presto – my splits drop. My last two were my fastest – almost 30 seconds faster than my second repeat.

When I'm in a race my thoughts expand to the runners around me – I pay attention to see if anyone is about to surge – who's struggling – who is strong – or if I'm along, who can I work on catching ahead of me. It's not exactly mystical – it's just about focusing on the task at hand – which at times can be more important than anything in my performance. My time meditating has helped me to improve my running and get more out of it.

SUNDAY, MARCH 8, 2009
PHASE 4: WEEK 4 OF 5

Well, we had a sixty degree change in the weather from Wednesday to Saturday on the east coast. The ten degree temperature on Wednesday highlighted how much "fun" it is to train for a spring marathon and the 70+ degree temp this weekend reminded me how few weeks I have left before Boston – only six short weeks from tomorrow – and two of those weeks will be spent basically resting.

Sitting here next to an open window, it's hard to believe that I had to postpone my first hard run this week because of snow. I was pretty happy with the workout - but the postponement left a few days less to recover before today.

I had the 'great" idea of running the tempo sections on the C&O canal path and the easy 10 mile section on the Appalachian trail. Well, I'm convinced that the mile markers on the C&O are a little long. There's no way I was running as slowly as my watch claimed. And I expected tough going on the Appalachian trail – but not nearly the ankle breaking sharp rocks that Brennan and I experienced. We ran ~6 miles in 50 minutes – and that might have been generous. There were some great views – but it was hard to appreciate since we were afraid to look up from the treacherous footing.

All of that blabbering is the long way of saying that the workout didn't go very well today. My tempo splits were way off – and I ended up cutting a couple miles off the run. No rest for the wicked this week – it's my last week over 90 miles. I only have one workout with tempo, but it's a doozy.

Yes, I know what you're thinking – "could the bad workout be from overtraining?" Well – I'm pushing myself more than ever before – so it's possible. But I'm not going to worry too much unless Tuesday doesn't go well. I'm giving myself a pseudo day off tomorrow – so I should be recovered enough – and if not, I can push the workout to Wednesday.

THURSDAY, MARCH 12, 2009
QUOTE: EMIL ZATOPEK

"You can't climb up to the second floor without a ladder . . . When you set your aim too high and don't fulfill it, then your enthusiasm turns to bitterness. Try for a goal that's reasonable, and then gradually raise it. That's the only way to get to the top."

Easy for a guy who won the 5k, 10, and marathon in the same Olympics to say. But he has a very good point. – even more for those of us who run for purely recreational purposes. Yes – you have to put some pressure on yourself to run your best – but you have to be realistic of what you can do given your ability, time to train, age etc . . .

Back when I started this blog I laid out some goals for Boston. My "A" goal was to break 2:30 – but I was sure to include some less challenging goals - because you never know what's going to happen – or how your body is going to respond to training.

I won't make a final goal until after my half-marathon tune up on 3/21 – but my training so far seems to point to a 2:33-34. That would still be a PR – and I certainly would be happy about that kind of time. But it's very tempting to go for the sub 2:30 anyways. 2:29 might be only two minutes faster than 2:31 – but it sure sound a lot better. However, I've already tried foolishness like that at the 2007 NYC marathon and paid for it. I was right at 1:15 at the half and struggled through a 1:22 second half. I completely lost motivation for 3-4 months – gained 15 pounds – and have been trying to get back to that level of fitness ever since. Hopefully I've learned my lesson – to be completely honest with myself and what I'm ready to run on 4/20.

FRIDAY, MARCH 13, 2009
FAITH & REASON (DOUBT)

A brief warning – 90% of the following post has nothing to do with running – rather it is related to the TV show "Lost", Jim Cramer vs. John Stewart, and Descartes. I blame Brian Godsey's blog for putting me in a philosophical frame of mind. You've been warned – so here it goes.

I consider myself a "man of reason." I feel like most of the world's problems are caused because people are appealing to faith rather than reason. The quote on my google page today was from the writer Norman Mailer – "Any war that requires the suspension of reason for support is a bad war." It alarms me how often people rely on emotion, faith, or pure momentum to make choices in this world. In my mind it's a major reason we find ourselves in an unpopular war and a major recession. As a society we suspended reason – or more specifically doubt – both at home and abroad for the last decade.

How is doubt related to reason? The famous "I think therefore I am" is taken from Descartes' "Meditations." There is a line of philosophical thought that posits we cannot even be sure of our own existence because we cannot trust our senses. Our senses are our only window to the world – and yet we know they can be tricked – so how do we know if the world or even we exist? So, Descartes says – if I can even doubt the existence of the world – is there anything I can't doubt?" He decided that he couldn't doubt that he is was doubting – and if he's doubting then he must exist. So, everything else that we call the universe might not exist – but at least I can confidently say that I exist, because I think (doubt).

The central conflict in "Lost" is between faith and reason. The character Locke represents faith, and Jack represents reason. The arc of the plot is a see-saw battle between the values of faith and the values of reason – this season the values of faith appear to be winning out. All the characters are ignoring any doubts they might have – all for different reasons. Jack & Locke represent the struggle that we have within ourselves. We need reason/doubt so we don't overextend ourselves – and we need faith to get out of bed in the morning. In the end – as much as I fight for more reason in the world – I understand that we need both.

Jim Cramer, of CNBC's "Mad Money" was on Jon Stewart last night. They didn't say one word about religion – but it was about how Jim Cramer had so much faith in the financial system – and how he, and others like him, communicated that faith to the marketplace. This complete lack of doubt or reason had led us to overextend ourselves. Stewart's point is that journalism should be about doubt – not cheerleading. But how do we get ourselves out of this recession? Eventually enough people will have to have some faith – hopefully along with a lot of reason – and take a chance.

So now for the 10% about running. When I started planning for the Boston marathon last summer – wasn't that an act of faith? There was no way I could have known exactly what would happen over the six months of training that was focused on the marathon. I had to take at least a little leap of faith – that my body would hold up – that I would still be interested in it six months later etc . . . The great thing about making these leaps of faith about your own behavior is that it feels good when you can make them become real. As important as doubt is – it is rarely accompanied by those same feelings – although without reason it would be impossible to make dreams real.

It's complicated.

SUNDAY, MARCH 15, 2009
PHASE 4: WEEK 5 OF 5

This last week was a slight decrease in intensity and mileage. I actually felt pretty good on my long run today. It marked the last of my four hardest weeks of training for Boston. I averaged almost 96 miles per week over the last four weeks.

This week is the last week of my fourth "phase." Other than the fact that Boston is only five weeks from tomorrow – it means that Saturday is my "tune-up" race – the National Half-marathon in DC. I'm looking to average 5:30's – which works out to ~1:12:00. The course does have some hills – so if I'm a little off pace I won't be too upset.

FRIDAY, MARCH 20, 2009
THE RACE COMETH

Well – the big one is exactly one month away. But I have my hardest planned effort to date tomorrow morning. I thought it would be a good chance to go over some of the race advice in "Lore of Running" by Tim Noakes. I'll go over some of the advice in the other books that I've been using for my training as I get closer to Boston.

The day before competition:

DRIVE OVER THE COURSE FOR A FINAL TIME, PAYING SPECIAL ATTENTION TO THE LAST SECTION OF THE RACE.

Well, these days you don't need to drive because most races have a youtube of the course online. I've watched the National course about 3-4 times – including once today. It's flat at the beginning – a steady hill from 5-8 miles and generally downhill after that. So I'm not looking for even splits.

EAT WISELY

The main message here is to not have any GI issues. I made sure to include some protein tonight – but not much sugar. I had a small steak, broccoli, wheat French bread, crackers, and toast with peanut butter and honey for "dessert."

ASSEMBLE YOUR RUNNING GEAR THE NIGHT BEFORE AND ENSURE THAT YOU HAVE EVERYTHING

Complete – except that I just remembered I need to attach my chip to my shoe.

GET ADEQUATE REST

Right after I'm done typing this I'll be off to bed. Of course it's going to be difficult with a 7am race that's 40 miles away. I'm planning on heading out the door at 5am.

The Day of the Race

WAKE UP CORRECTLY

There is nothing correct about a 4:45am wake-up call. The author talks about finding a way to wake up "gradually." I fear if I don't heed my watch alarm right away I'm not going to make it up.

DRESS APPROPRIATELY FOR RACE CONDITIONS

This will be tricky tomorrow. It's supposed to be 32 degrees at 7am. If you're going to check your warm-up clothing you pretty much have to only have on your racing gear for at least 15 minutes before the race (the last call to the line). So I went to Walmart and bought some cheap sweats that I can throw away at the start. Most races know people will do this – so they'll collect the sweats after the race and give them to the poor. As for the actual race, I'm going to go with just my singlet – and as my wife calls them – "man panties." However, I'm going to wear gloves and a winter hat to start out. I'll abandon those within the first few miles.

MAKE YOUR PRERACE MEAL A WINNER

It's the same basic idea as the meal the day before the race. Don't eat anything that will put your stomach in knots – or worse . . . Also, coffee is a good idea. I started drinking coffee before races in college – it seems to work pretty well for longer races.

I'm planning on eating a Dunkin Donuts egg-white flat bread breakfast sandwich tomorrow morning. I know that sounds odd – but it's pretty light on the stomach. That and of course a cup of joe.

ALLOW YOURSELF AMPLE WARM-UP TIME

I plan on being there at least an hour before the race. I'll probably jog easily for about 10 minutes – 40-50 minutes before the race. Do some good stretching – more dynamic rather than static. I also have another pre-race habit I learned in college – I lay still – close my eyes and imagine a red liquid filling my body from my feet to my head. Then I imagine the liquied turning blue – again starting from my feet to my head. The effect is that I'm relaxing every muscle in my body. I may run a few strides as well – to get my muscles ready to run fast. I'll also try to have a cup of water that I can take small sips from – the nerves can lead to a little cotton mouth sometimes.

That's it! Time to get some rest.

SUNDAY, MARCH 22, 2009
PHASE 5: WEEK 1 OF 4

I'm finally entering the final phase of my training for Boston. During these final four weeks (have I written "final" enough in the last two sentences?) I'm going to try to post more frequently than I have recently – focusing on the history and uniqueness of the Boston Marathon. I'll also have a lot to say about what has worked in my training and where I've struggled.

Whatever happens four weeks from tomorrow – I know that my training has improved my fitness to a level I haven't seen for a while. How do I know that? Yesterday was my first real test since my training started in November. I ran the National Half-marathon in DC – although it was cold (~30 degrees at the start) and an early morning (7am) – the wind was pretty much non-existent. I started out with the lead group of marathoners – our first mile was 5:29 – which was about what I planned to average over the 13.1 miles. As we descended down East Capital Ave to The Mall the group picked up the pace a little – our second mile was ~5:20.

Although I missed the 3rd & 4th mile markers – I could tell that they were picking the pace up even faster. I didn't quite feel comfortable running 5:15's. So I backed off the pace a little around 3.5 miles into the race. Around the 5 mile mark we started to ascend gradually – through these hills my mile splits slowed to between 5:30-5:40. After the seven mile mark the course started downhill again. I knew that the significant hills were pretty much over. I started to push the pace. My splits went back down to ~5:20 – with my 10th mile at a 5:06 (the marker certainly could have been off). I was 53:45 through 10 miles. I usually fall apart in ½ marathons after the 10 mile mark – but I felt strong. I was able to average a little over 5:20 in the last three miles – coming through at 1:10:36.

A week ago I said I'd be happy with a 1:12:00. Then I had a confidence boosting workout on Tuesday that made me thing that a sub 1:11:00 was reasonable. This is really the best that I imagined myself running when I started this crazy trip back in November. There are so many things that can go wrong in marathon training. So far, knock on wood, the training seems to be working out perfectly – pushing me to my highest level of fitness without leaving me stale or injured.

Next is the "easy" part. I have two more weeks of decent training (although lower mileage than my fourth phase) and then the wonderful taper.

More evidence that this training plan is good preparation for the marathon is the performance of Brennan Feldhausen yesterday. He ran a very strong 2:42 for his first marathon ever. Brennan and I have been running a lot of our training together – and we certainly have a similar philosophy. He not only ran a good time – he looked very strong doing it. Hopefully next month I can execute as well as he did yesterday. Great job Brennan!

This week is a little step up in mileage. The first few days will be pretty easy as I recover from yesterday. I'm planning a massage on Tuesday to get the kinks worked out. Then it's back to business on Wednesday with a long tempo workout – and my last 20+ miler this weekend.

MONDAY, MARCH 22, 2009
WELL, DO YA PUNK?

Staring down a .44 in the hands of Dirty Harry – and not being quite sure how many shots he's fired – that's about how I feel planning on going sub-2:30 at Boston. But given my half-marathon time this last weekend – I think it's time to seriously consider it.

There is a race split calculator that's specifically designed for the Boston course that I found online. They ask for your goal time, age, gender, and recent race time. They give you back approximate mile splits which take into consideration the infamous hills of the course. It also gives you a "predicted" time – based on the recent race times. Here is what it spit out for me.

MILES	GOAL TIME	SPLIT	PREDICTED TIME	SPLIT
1.0	5:32	5:32	5:26	5:26
2.0	11:11	5:39	10:59	5:33
3.0	16:48	5:36	16:31	5:31
4.0	22:21	5:32	21:58	5:27
5.0	28:10	5:49	27:42	5:43
6.0	33:52	5:41	33:18	5:35
7.0	39:33	5:41	38:53	5:35
8.0	45:23	5:49	44:37	5:43
9.0	51:04	5:40	50:12	5:34
10.0	56:52	5:48	55:55	5:42
11.0	1:02:41	5:48	1:01:37	5:42
12.0	1:08:23	5:41	1:07:13	5:35
13.0	1:14:05	5:42	1:12:50	5:36
14.0	1:19:48	5:42	1:18:27	5:37
15.0	1:25:38	5:50	1:24:11	5:44
16.0	1:31:09	5:31	1:29:37	5:25
17.0	1:37:04	5:55	1:35:26	5:49

18.0	1:42:57	5:52	1:41:12	5:46
19.0	1:48:39	5:42	1:46:49	5:37
20.0	1:54:30	5:50	1:52:34	5:44
21.0	2:00:34	6:03	1:58:31	5:57
22.0	2:06:08	5:34	2:04:00	5:28
23.0	2:11:46	5:38	2:09:33	5:32
24.0	2:17:26	5:39	2:15:07	5:34
25.0	2:23:04	5:38	2:20:39	5:32
26.0	2:28:49	5:44	2:26:18	5:38
26.2	2:29:59	1:10	2:27:28	1:09

So, should I?

WEDNESDAY, MARCH 25, 2009
AN ANNIVERSARY

Early last Saturday morning I woke up with a start – I looked over at the clock, it was 3:15am. I still had over an hour to sleep before my alarm went off to make the drive down to RFK in DC for the half-marathon. My nerves, however, wouldn't let me get those extra z's. But it was a good nervousness. I was feeling confident in my training – I knew I was ready for a fast one that day. My confidence also reminded me that an anniversary of sorts was around the corner.

I started thinking about my senior year of college. There was about a six-week period starting in February until the end of March of that year when everything seemed to go right where my running was concerned. I won the 3k and 5k at indoor conference (MCC – now Horizon League). Then on March 25th I competed in the 10k at the Alabama Relays.

It's not that this was really an important meet. I don't remember being especially nervous about it. I do remember starting out with the lead pack – feeling very relaxed. I remember my assistant coach on the back stretch calling out my splits every lap. I remember that my first 5k split was ~15:15 – which was on pace for a big PR. I then remember feeling stronger as I went through the second 5k – soon I was running on my own – the laps falling away – not that there wasn't effort – but it wasn't a forced effort – it felt natural.

As I came down to the final laps my coach seemed to be getting excited. I don't quite remember when he started telling me I had a shot at going under 30 minutes – but I do remember him yelling with 600 meters to go that I needed a 65 second last lap for a sub-30 minute 10k. It sounds ridiculous now (I can hardly run one lap at 65 seconds these days) – but somehow I found something extra – sprinting that last lap as hard as I could. As I crossed the finish line I looked over at my coach – who was running towards me along with a half dozen teammates. He was yelling "you were under!" Soon my teammates were piling on me – like I had made the last second shot in the NCAA basketball tournament.

Although I had some changes to run faster that year – including at the Penn Relays – I never got within 40 seconds of that time. I guess that in some ways I keep running to recreate that "one shining moment." I'll never come close to running that fast for 10k again – but the great thing about running is that I can find new goals – and feel just as good about meeting the new goals as I did on that cool March evening 10 years ago today.

Man, I'm getting old.

THURSDAY, MARCH 26, 2009
THE DAY AFTER A HARD WORKOUT

One of the more significant additions that I've made to my training for Boston is what I do the day after a hard workout.

Nine of the last 12 weeks I've run a 13-15 miles the day after a hard workout. I've never done this before. It seems to help both physically and mentally. Physically, my body is having to adapt to a relatively long run when it's already depleted. But I think the most positive effect is psychological. Even though the pace isn't too fast – it feels like I've accomplished something when I look at my watch and see that I've run 90+ minutes in the middle of the week.

Although I haven't been posting it on my blog – I've been lifting weights on most of these days as well. It's nice to have a different physical activity to mix things up a little – and my wife thanks me for not wasting away completely.

SATURDAY, MARCH 28, 2009
THE PACKET ARRIVES!

Get ready for over three weeks of minutiae that you may or may not care about :) With that warning – my race packet for Boston came this week!

The packet includes race bib pick-up card with my bib number (1143) and other information. Most importantly, it includes the 22 page program book with schedule of events, expo info, race start area info, "course amenities", finish area info, and beautiful maps to every important geographic area related to the marathon. There is also a booklet on "proper hydration" and of course, another booklet with overpriced (though, I'm sure I'll buy something) merchandise.

Over the next three weeks I'll review every detail. Not that it will necessarily help on race day – but it will somehow make me feel better. Although my first quick read did raise a few questions: 1) How am I getting to the start? The program book makes it seem like the start line is blocked off for a five mile radius – unless you take the shuttle. But you're supposed to be on the shuttle by 7am, which wouldn't be so bad, except that it's a 10am race. This is one of the many details that I'll rely on others who have run the race to help me decide what I do. 2) It looks like I have to be at my corral by 9:10 (50 minutes before the race) – how crowded will it be? Is there room to jog around like there was at New York? Are there porta-johns at the corrals? 3) They have water stops every mile. I don't think I should take water every mile – but how often should I? I guess it depends on the weather – but I should put together some kind of plan.

To be continued . . .

SUNDAY, MARCH 29, 2009
PHASE 5: WEEK 2 OF 4

Last week was a pretty good week. I was able to recover from my half and keep up the intensity. The workout on Wednesday wasn't as fast as some of the workouts we've done – but it was on a deceivingly rolling trail around BWI airport. It was also a 22 mile day on a work day, four days after a hard half-marathon.

One way to gauge my fitness is that I was actually looking forward to the run today. Arjun, Ryan, Zero, Kris and myself started at Druid Hill Park – one of the oldest planned parks in the US (1860). The hills in the park are rough – but it gets even worse as you run north on Greenspring Avenue, near Pimlico race track and into Baltimore County. The total distance (22 miles) & hills were tough – but we added 8 X 5.5 minutes at tempo with one minute rest for good measure. This workout came straight from Jack Daniels' book – probably the most important purchase I've made in my marathon preparation.

The idea was to run hills so big that anything on the Boston course would feel like "love bumps." From the looks of bitterness on the faces of my friends today – I think the mission was accomplished. Although Ryan had some cramping issues – everybody ran well.

So what now? The number of miles and intensity drop a little this week. I've got another 2X3 mile workout that I'll probably do at the airport again. Next Saturday is a "dress rehearsal" of sorts. The goal is to run 15 miles at marathon pace. After that day, I'll only have one more run over 10 miles before Boston. I feel very lucky to have made it this far without injuries (knock on wood) or just feeling overwhelmed by the training.

WEDNESDAY, APRIL 1, 2009
ARMY 10 MILER

Such is distance running that you have to look forward to the next goal before you've completed the current one. Registration opened today for the Army 10 miler. I'm excited because it's a relatively fast course and I think the distance is a little more natural for me than the marathon. It will be fun to focus a little less on running long runs and a little more on speed.

So do I have a plan after that? Well, yes I do. I'd like to run a fast 5k or 10k on the track next spring and then find a flat and "fast" marathon for the Fall of 2010. Beyond that – I'm not sure. I have a slight itch to try my hand at the triathlon – but we'll see. Do they allow arm floaties in the swim?

SATURDAY, APRIL 4, 2009
QUOTE OF THE DAY: ONCE A RUNNER

This is an excerpt from the chapter in "Once a Runner" by John L. Parker Jr., where the main character, Cassidy, is staring a third "set" of 20 X 400m @ 62-63 seconds. Basically 15 miles worth of running at 4:08-4:12 pace. A little unbelievable – but something you have to push reality a little to get at a deeper truth.

"He began the melancholy ritual as night was falling. After the first five he was running by the soft glow of a huge clear moon. Cassidy thought, Bruce thinks of everything.

Then he sought out the mental neutrality that is the refuge the contained wan comfort of the runner. He grooved his mind upon the thin platinum rail of his task, a line that stretched out in front of him and disappeared into the gloom, further than he could contemplate all at once, even if he had the desire to, which he did not. When his trance broke and a word or phrase popped into his mind, his dizzy mind played with it like a seal with a beach ball, in a disturbing, gibberishly mad way, the way your mind acts in the druggy twilight before sleep. In a very controlled, abstract way, he knew how much he was suffering; the slightest break in this concentration allowed self-pity to well up in him instantly.

He was, in a manner of speaking, accustomed to this distress the same manner that a boxer is 'accustomed' to being struck; but the familiarity of experience in no way lessens the blow or mitigates its physiological effects. It merely provides the competitor a backdrop against which his current travail may be played, gives him a certain serenity in the face of otherwise overwhelming stimuli, allows dispassionate insight where otherwise there would be only a rush of panic. In a hail of killing blows, the fighter's quiet center of logic, schooled in brutality, will be calmly theorizing: We are hurt pretty badly. If we do not cover up and take up the slack we will soon be unconscious.

Not that this quite center of logic fears unconsciousness (indeed, how welcome it might seem at times), but it know that one can't win while unconscious. Likewise, no highly trained runner slacks off because he fears pain, but because the quiet center of logic says he will win nothing if he runs himself to a standstill.

All of this availed Cassidy not at all. His deeply ingrained conditioning and his mahogany-hard legs merely allowed him to push himself that much more. He had the mental ability to literally run himself right into the ground like Sambo's tiger. He knew that Denton expected him to do exactly that, and, just as each repetition made the next seem more impossible, he knew that without question he WOULD do it. There was no refuge in injury, his body could not be injured in this way. There was no refuge in mercy, there was nothing to forgive, no one to issue dispensation. And at last he saw: There was no refuge in cowardice, because he was not afraid. There was no alternative, it just had to be DONE."

MONDAY, APRIL 6, 2009
PHASE 5: WEEK 3 OF 4

The taper starts now.

My "dress rehearsal" on Saturday wasn't exactly what I hoped for – but even with a strong wind, I felt strong as the run progressed. With a smart taper, a little added adrenaline, and good luck with the weather I still think I have a chance of sub 2:30 – but it's gonna be tough.

This week brings a little sanity to my running schedule and diverse weather. I'm writing this from The Twin Cities – where I'll be working through Thursday. Then Friday, Kendra and I head down to Orlando for a few days. It's hard to believe that a little less than a week after I come back from Florida I'll be heading to Boston. It's been a long time coming. Over the last 22 weeks (the first week of November, when I "officially" started my Boston training) I've run over 1,700 miles or an average of almost 78 miles per week. The barn is bursting with hay – now I just need to rest and eat smart.

MONDAY, APRIL 12, 2009
PHASE 5: WEEK 4 OF 4

Here we are boys and girls – the final week.

I was hoping to post more over the last few weeks before Boston – but instead I seem to be posting less. I was in Minneapolis Sunday through Thursday for work – it wasn't a hugely stressful week – but it was pretty busy. And I spent the last few days in Orlando (or "The Do" as my wife and I now call it). Actually it's probably the best that I have some downtime from thinking about Boston. This blog has been helpful from the perspective of keeping my motivation up – but as my high school coach used to say about me – "Ben, sometimes you analyze until you paralyze."

During my taper – the most important thing for me will be rest and nutrition. More on that tomorrow.

It's amazing that I only have one more week until Boston. That's the crazy thing about marathon running – it requires such a long cycle of training that the day is magnified even more greatly than it would be otherwise.

MONDAY, APRIL 13, 2009
THE TAPER

Many of you are fully aware of the concept of the taper – but I thought I'd write a little about it.

Most of this content is from "Lore of Running", by Tim Noakes MD – with some help from Jack Daniels and Pete Pfitzinger.

The taper is that somewhat counter intuitive concept that the last few weeks before a goal competition you should reduce the amount of training volume and intensity. The idea is that you cannot perform at the highest level while training at the volume necessary to develop your different systems (circulatory, muscular, etc.) for the race. You actually need to give your body a break that is long enough to let it recover and short enough that you don't lose any fitness.

Volume and Intensity:
The standard period for a taper is two weeks – although the highest volume weeks are probably at least 4-6 weeks before the goal competition. Experts usually suggest running 50% of the highest mileage two weeks out and 30-40% the week before. There is some debate regarding intensity – some say that you should retain intense workouts – just decreasing volume – others say you should cut out intensity completely in the last 10 days before major competition. My plan is somewhat in-between – I am running a track workout tomorrow – but it's much easier than any "hard" workouts I've run recently. I'm also running 4-6 100 meter accelerations most days to keep my legs fresh.

Nutrition:
It's as important to stay on track with nutrition during this period as any other period of training. Somebody like me, who puts on weight pretty

easily, needs to steer clear of sweets and fat. I have to say that I didn't do great last week, being on the road, but I think that it will be easier this week at home.

Another nutritional suggestion that Noakes makes is to have a very high carbohydrate load regimen in the last 3-7 days before competition (he suggest 500g per day of complex carbohydrates per day). He also discusses the pros and cons of including a carbohydrate depletion phase 7-10 days before competition. This phase is meant to "starve" the system of carbs, which is supposed to make the body more likely to retain carbs during the load phase. But there is some disagreement on the effectiveness of the depletion phase and whether it might actually be harmful. I didn't really do the depletion phase :)

Mental Energy:
Noakes also writes about "storing creative energy" by avoiding creative activities the last few days before the race. That's one nice thing about Boston being on Monday – I have at least two days without working before the race. I'll probably bring a book along and read most of the time.

Noakes writes of a "colleague who missed one ultra-marathon because of influenza now refuses to work for the last 7 days before a race. When not running during this period, he dons a surgical mask, takes leave of his family, and cloisters himself in a sterile environment, accompanied only by a library of Eastern philosophy. At such times only those who are known to be free of marathon-destroying germs have access to him." Then Noakes writes that this shouldn't be thought of as odd behavior – since Noakes did write a book just shy of 800 pages on running I think he might be a little blinded from what most people would consider odd.

Another part of the mental preparation for a goal race is mentally rehearsing the race. I'll talk through this a little later this week – when I go over my race plan.

One week to go! Current weather report for Boston on 4/20 – low of 41 and a high of 53 – 30% chance of showers. Not beach weather, but great marathoning weather!

Endurance: Blog of a Distance Runner and Triathlete

WEDNESDAY, APRIL 15, 2009
HANSONS-BROOKS BOSTON PREVIEW

Hansons-Brooks Distance Project is one of the more interesting American distance running group to surface in the last ten years. They specialize in taking post-collegiate runners and making them pretty darn good marathoners. Of course, they helped Brian Sell to be an Olympian and took seven of the top 22 places at Boston in 2006. That they are from my home state and that one of my oldest friends runs for them is just icing on the cake.

On their site they are posting interviews with each of the six runners participating at Boston – as well as the two coaches and founders of the group – Kevin and Keith Hanson. The interview with Kevin and Keith Hanson helps to shed some light on why Boston is so special and why group training is so important. The topic of how groups can bring out the best in individuals is so interesting to me that I think it will be the focus of my blog after Boston.

The other interview that interests me is with one of the oldest friends and high school teammate – Todd Snyder. Todd and I go way back – as in – we were in the same cub scout troop growing up. We eventually got into running at different middle schools in Ann Arbor, MI. In high school we both ran for Pioneer High School. Todd was an okay runner our freshman year – but as our sophomore year went by he started getting better and better.

We convinced him to train during the next summer. After that, I was lucky to see him at any point after the first 800 meters of a race. He won six individual state titles (XC, indoor, outdoor) – basically unbeaten in races for our high school his last two years. Michigan is a pretty deep running state. Todd beat some pretty impressive dudes – including Abdul Alzindani (a year younger than us, but who eventually was Foot Locker National Champion) to win his individual titles.

Todd went on to the University of Michigan – where he places 10th at XC D1 National – an All-American stud. Although his talent is pretty amazing – he is even a better person. We became pretty good friends by our junior year – and except for the period where he dated my sister (don't ask) – we've been good friends ever since. He's just a good all-around guy – someone who gives more than he takes – a kind spirit.

Anyways – enough gushing – it sounds like he's in shape to pull a great performance next week. Although he didn't tell me – I heard from other sources that he was in 2:14 shape last fall until he had a stress fracture in his foot that kept him out of Chicago. So I'm guessing that he got back into similar shape. In their interview – Kevin and Keith seem to be a little secretive about what they think he can do – which sounds promising to me. I talked to him last week and he seem to feel confident in his fitness.

Good luck Todd and the rest of the Hansons crew!

UPDATE: I just read a Q&A with Brian Sell on the Runners World website – he is pretty high on Todd:

"A guy on our team to watch is Todd Snyder. He's run like 2:20. We just did our simulator run the other day, our 16-miler, and he ran the equivalent of a 2:12. He's definitely fit."

I also liked Sell's quote about Dathan Ritzenhein. "Just looking at him five years ago, I just thought he was this Nike-sponsored punk who did a couple of yoga exercises and ran 30 miles a week and just was so talented that he was able to pull stuff out like that."

THURSDAY, APRIL 16, 2009
THE PLAN

My college coach, Gordon Thomson, used to say "plan the race and race the plan." Yes, you can't freak out if circumstances force you to change plans – but you need to go into a race understanding your goal with a realistic plan of how you will get there. In some ways, I've been doing this on a macro level with my training plan – and as with my training plan I've learned a few things in my four marathons that will help me on Monday.

Probably the most important part of the plan is pacing. Because of the unique elevation profile of the Boston course, the history, and the strong fan support in some places on the course (Wellesley College, Cleveland Circle, etc.) there is probably no other course on earth with as much thought that has gone into mileage splits than Boston. I thought about taping the splits onto my arm from one of the pacing calculators that I wrote about in a previous post – but I'm worried that I might rely on it too much. But I do think the calculators were helpful because they told me that even on the biggest downhill mile I shouldn't go any faster than 5:30 and that I shouldn't go any slower on the up-hillls than slightly over six minutes per mile.

For me, the biggest trick will be the first few miles. At New York in 2007, my second mile (coming down the bridge) was under 5:20 pace. I was having way too much fun – feeling the excitement of the race and I paid for it later. This time I'm planning to have the disposition of a monk. I almost want to feel groggy the first few miles – like I'm slowly waking up as the race unfolds. The first four miles are like running down a sledding hill – in my training I sought out hills like those and concentrated on flowing down them – focusing on keeping my stride short to keep the pounding to a minimum.

Although I will be keeping mile splits – the first split that I'll really pay attention to is the 10th mile. I'm hoping to be somewhere around 57 minutes. I've heard it said that the marathon is best broken into thirds – the first ten miles, the second ten miles, and the last 10k. These are the splits where I'll really take stock of how I'm doing. I'm hoping that my second 10 miles will also be close to 57 minutes – leaving me a 36 minute 10k to break 2:30.

Another big part of "the plan" is nutrition. I discovered Roctane Gu's – which is the best gel that I've ever used. It really provides a kick – we'll probably learn that it has some illegal chemical in it that will take 10 years off my life – but hey, I'm trying to break 2:30! I'm going to take one Roctane 15 minutes before the race starts and three more during the race (miles 8, 16, and 22). Boston is the only race I know of that has water/Gatorade stops at every mile. So there shouldn't be a problem with hydration. I'll probably take water and Gatorade every 2-3 miles.

The other parts of the plan are related to pre-race. I arrive in Boston on Saturday. I plan on sleeping in on Sunday, and except for a 30 minute shakeout run, the expo, and dinner – I'm going to be laying around watching TV or reading a book.

I'll have to leave for the bus at ~6am on Monday morning. I'll bring a bunch of clothing and maybe a cheap poncho. They force you to check your bag at least an hour before the start. So I'll bring some warm clothes that I'll just throw away at the start (they give the clothing to charity). The forecast is for low to mid 40's and a 30% chance of rain – ok for racing, but not waiting around. In terms of the actual race, the worst part of the forecast is for a 15 mph wind coming out of the east, which just happens to be the direction we'll be running for 26.2 miles. At least, it's better than 80 degrees and sunny like it has been some years.

FRIDAY, APRIL 17, 2009
THE FLOW

One part of the preparation that I haven't really talked about is mental imagery. I can remember in college looking at a course map every Friday night during XC season and imagining myself running strongly from start to finish.

I might sound like an odd thing to do – but I don't know of a good coach who doesn't have his athletes use this technique. It works because when you toe the line you feel like you've already been there – you've already run this course strongly. And that extra bit of confidence allows you to react to the difficult parts of the race in a more positive manner. You're less likely to give up – you're more able to relax and push through the difficult times.

One powerful image for me is a flowing river. It may be calm, but there is a lot of force and it is continually moving. Of course there is a lot of flowing going on when you're running. All the thousands of miniature "rivers" delivering oxygen to your muscles and removing toxins. The air moving in and out of your lungs. The wind flowing around your body.

To etch that imagery into my head – I ran down to a portion of Jones Falls, which runs along the Southern end of Falls Road here in Baltimore. Even though it's only ½ mile from Penn Station and next to I-83 – it's very peaceful there. I ran my last six striders in a quiet section between two mini "rapids." I thought about how the rocks and boulders were like the Newton hills – and how the water just flowed over or around the rocks easily. The rocks could not stop the water – they could only give the water a voice and texture.

Boston is of course a fun race for mental imagery – the crowds, the landmarks, the hills. This route is better known than the actual road that

Pheidippides traveled from Marathon to Athens all those years ago. The Boston course is full of heroes and villains – comedy and tragedy – joy and sorrow. The course itself is a celebration of life lived intensely and deliberately.

On Monday I might be in too much pain to think of running the course in any poetic sense – but I hope that I can at least draw some inspiration from the place – so that I can perform my best.

I've probably spent enough time analyzing the race :) So this will probably be my last post before Monday. Thanks to everyone for their support and good luck to everyone running on Monday!

MONDAY, APRIL 20, 2009
READY FOR A BURGER AND A BEER

It's odd writing this thinking that my journey that I started in November is now over. It's not a bad thing necessarily – I'm happy to have a little more free time and eat some very bad food for a few weeks :)

I'm fairly happy with my overall time – given that we had a 10-15 mph head wind for 26.2 miles. I'll write something a little more detailed tomorrow – just thought I'd post something for anyone interested in my total time and/or splits.

Mile 1	5:48	Mile 14	5:43
Mile 2	5:36	Mile 15	5:48
Mile 3	5:36	Mile 16	5:32
Mile 4	5:33	Mile 17	(missed a mile split giving my friend
Mile 5	5:47	Mile 18	Melissa a high-five) 11:45 for 2 miles
Mile 6	5:41	Mile 19	5:43
Mile 7	5:45	Mile 20	5:54 (1:54:34 for 20 miles)
Mile 8	5:48	Mile 21	6:10 (Heartbreak Hill)
Mile 9	5:46	Mile 22	5:46
Mile 10	5:45	Mile 23	6:07
Mile 11	5:41	Mile 24	5:55
Mile 12	5:40	Mile 25	6:16
Mile 13	5:43	Mile 26.2	7:47 (1.2 miles) Total Time: 2:32.35

TUESDAY, APRIL 21, 2009
THE RACE

My first conscious moments of April 20th, 2009 were sometime around 1-2am. I woke up in the middle of the night as I normally do before a big race. My sub-conscious seemed to be pleading with me to be cautious – as my first thoughts were regarding the Miami Half-Marathon I ran in January. I ended up running with a marathoner for a few miles – and as I turned off to the finish I had pangs of guilt and sympathy as I realized he had many painful miles ahead of him.

Today I would be switching places with that runner. The only thing that could at least buffer the pain I had in front of me was to be smart at the beginning. The start of a major marathon is like the beginning of youthful love. You want to throw yourself into it fully – not thinking about the consequences or the possible pain that your thoughtlessness might cause in the future. As those of certain age know – the wisdom and maturity is born from pain that follows such foolishness.

My second awakening was at 5:20am. I drove to a T stop and rode it to the Boston Commons where I would catch a bus to the start at Hopkinton. The bus ride was another reminder to be cautious. The ride takes close to an hour and has all the riders asking "I have to run all the way back?"

I found a relatively empty set of porta-johns. Not to be too graphic, but along with eating right – making sure that you are as "empty" as possible is a big key to having a good race. I quickly found my friends and we joked and laughed as we lay on the wet grass. The area eventually became so crowded that I decided to head for the buses where I would drop off my gear bag. In it was warm clothing, my training shoes, a little money and my cell phone.

I walked down with others to the start at the town square of Hopkinton (population <15,000). The area had the feel of a small town festival. I watched the women start at 9:30am. After some stretching and resting I walked over to my corral. Fortunately my qualifying time allowed me to get into the first corral behind the elites.

As I sat, stretched, and sipped on some water a volunteer asked me if it was my first Boston. We chatted a little bit and she told me that the elites were going to pass right on the other side of the French barricades beside me. Apparently they used to bring the elites through the cemetery – but some of them complained that it was bad luck. So they changed the route so that they passed next to the first few corrals of runners.

10-15 minutes before the start I saw Hall, Cheriyot, Sell, and others come towards me. Both Hall and Sell were very pumped – they high-fived us as they passed. Then my friend Todd Snyder came by – he was in the zone – and I had to shout his name a few times before he looked up and noticed me.

Several minutes later the gun fired and we were off. The first few miles were a blur – but I stayed pretty relaxed. The road was crowded – but I was able to run my pace without being blocked or pushed.

As the miles went by runners started to coalesce into groups – like a stream of water forming droplets. These groups were formed, in part, because of the wind. People were less willing to run by themselves. I had promised myself that I wouldn't freak out if I found myself by my lonesome. I was able to do some drafting – but I didn't surge to the next group when I found myself alone – I just tried to keep the same level of effort.

My first 10 miles were very close to my goal of 57 minutes. That first hour of running was spent running through small towns and longer stretches of woodlands, over creeks, and alongside ponds. In more open areas near the ponds it was evident that the #1 opponent for the day would be the wind. It wasn't a blow you over wind – but it did provide some additional drag.

Around the 12-mile mark was the infamous "scream tunnel" at Wellesley College. It was pretty crazy – they take their unofficial responsibility as the cheerleading squad of the Boston marathon pretty seriously.

The next major milestone was the halfway mark – 1:14:48. Although I knew that I was about 30-40 seconds slower than I had hoped – I felt strongly that I could run a faster second half. Usually in a marathon I'm questioning what I got myself into at the halfway point – so my confidence was a good sign.

Since the 10 mile mark, I had been 20-30 seconds back of a big group. My plan was to pass them by mile 15 – but I hadn't made much of a dent. In the second half of the 15th mile, there was a long downhill to the Charles River – a downhill that belies what's to come. The bridge over the Charles River was a bridge to pain – within a few steps after the bridge I was on my way up the first of the four Newton hills.

The group that I had stalked for the last five miles melted around me as I powered my way up the hill. I felt stronger after 16 miles than any other marathon I've run. At 17 miles was a slight downhill – I saw my friend Melissa cheering off to the side of the road. She was one familiar face in a sea of strangers. I went over to the side of the road and gave her a high five. In my distraction I missed the 17 mile mark – the only one I missed the entire marathon.

I hit 20 miles in 1:54:30 – just 30 seconds slower than I had planned. I felt strong enough at that point that I still thought I could edge under 2:30. Soon after came the infamous heartbreak hill. I've heard a lot of people say it's not that bad – but I certainly wasn't disappointed by the challenge.

Yes, most of the last five miles is downhill – but there are some rolling hills that I didn't expect. I still thought I had a shot of running under 2:30 until I got to the hill at mile 23. At that point, I knew it just wasn't in the cards. The wind worsened after heartbreak hill and my legs started to stiffen. I didn't completely throw in the towel – I tried to key off some other runners and finish strong – but I slowed pretty substantially in the last few miles. Given that I didn't have a shot of sub 2:30 I decided it was better to enjoy the crowds and the experience instead of killing myself the last few miles.

After crossing the finish line, I slowly made my way to the buses to get my gear bag. Every 15-20 feet a medical volunteer asked me if I needed any assistance. The Boston volunteers are the best of any race I've participated in – they love this day and give it their all to make a good experience for the runners.

Eventually I got a massage and a woman who thought her job was a good excuse to torture helpless runners, drained and cleaned out my blisters.

Overall the day was a great success. Yea – it would have been nice to not have such a strong headwind – but looking back on my first post outlining my goals – much more has gone right than has gone wrong since November.

Some people mistakenly believe that the marathon is an individual event. But I've been lucky to run with a very supportive group of people without whom I could never have PR'd today. And of course everybody who has offered their support in the comments on this blog and in person. It's been a great adventure. Thank you.

WEDNESDAY, APRIL 22, 2009
THE RECOVERY

Since I work from home and apparently have no life outside of running – the last two day have felt like I've been sick. There have been no long runs or two-a-days or hard workouts – just working, eating, drinking, and sleeping. Of course this is a good thing – but it's an odd adjustment. I can't even seem to get off my good nutritional habits as much as I hoped. Yes, I've had a few ice cream brownie sundaes and some good beer – but most of my meals are still straight out my plan that Melissa helped me with – what's the fun in that?!!

I've elevated my legs a few times and had a cold water bath last night. Next week, after my muscles have healed a little, I'm planning on a massage.

Tomorrow is my first run since the marathon. Given the amount of soreness that I have right now – I'm not sure that I'll be able to make it the planned four miles. We'll see.

In the longer term I'll be running only easy miles until June. My mileage will be increasing from 30 miles next week to 65 miles the last week of May. I'm trying to give myself plenty of time to recover – because from June through October I'm planning on a lot of intense training. Not as many miles as I've been running for Boston, but a larger percentage of hard mileage.

This doesn't have anything to do with my recovery – but I realized today that my time at the Miami Half-Marathon, which was planned to be at marathon pace, was only three seconds off the pace I ran at Boston. Miami was 1:16:19 and Boston was 2:32:35. Weird.

FRIDAY, MAY 1, 2009
WHAT'S NEXT?

Well, the name of my blog means I either need to stop posting, change the name, or start training for Boston 2010. I've decided on the middle path.

Although training will still be a focus of the blog – I want to explore a topic that interests me – group training. I have a Master's degree in Industrial/Organizational Psychology and my thesis was on how status of people within groups effect performance within that group. Also, I work for OptumHealth (sister company of UnitedHealthcare) – a company that delivers disease management, wellness programing, online wellness content etc. Basically we are trying to improve the health of our clients and consumers. And finally, I've been lucky to be a part of several groups/teams as a runner. These affiliations have always made me a better runner.

All of these experiences have led me to believe that group training is a very powerful tool in maximizing performance and fitness. In fact, I think it's the key to improving the low levels of fitness that we see in the US. We need to help people to form groups that meet regularly and support each other as they find out how to live healthier lives. I first started working in the health management field at the University of Michigan, at a research center directed by Dee Edington – who is one of the most respected people in his field. One concept that he discussed often was that improving health isn't just about lowering healthcare costs – it's about improving the "vitality" of our society.

SUNDAY, MAY 3, 2009
SUPREME VICTORY (OVER A NICE KID WITH CELIACS DISEASE)

It's been just under two weeks since Boston. I've run 43 miles in those last 13 days – a far cry from the end of February-March when I was running at least four times that amount in the same number of days. It is a good thing – my body needs to rest – the first day that I felt really "normal" was yesterday.

That being said – my mind isn't so ready to give way to this period of "rest." I have a bit of a competitive side – it's hard for me to sit on the sidelines when there are so many races in the area. So I registered for the "Making Tracks for Celiac 10k" here in Baltimore. In a compromise between my rational self and my competitive self, I planned on running more of an escalation workout than a true race. The plan was to start out at over six minute pace and drop down each mile so that I was only really running all out the last two miles – when I would let my competitive self take over and have some fun.

The race developed pretty much as I had hoped – except for the cold rain. My first mile was 6:08 – roughly the same pace as heartbreak hill at Boston – except a lot more comfortable ☺ The course was mostly within Patterson Park. A series of turnbacks and loops that made me want to keep the leaders in site so I would get lost. Over the next few miles my pace dropped to 5:53 and then the 5:40's. By now the 5k runners were long gone and I saw only one runner in front of me.

At mile four I really started to push the pace and I passed the leader soon after. Taking the lead can put you slightly off balance – because you no longer have someone in front of you to focus on. I was taught to always pass the leader with a surge – then they are much more likely to just let you go. The second place guy stayed close enough to hear his footsteps for about a half-mile and then I started to pull away. My last 2.2 miles were in 11:24 (about 5:10 pace).

It was nice to stretch out the legs a little, win a race, and get a little money. At least that's how I felt until the awards ceremony. As the MC announced the top 3 names he asked the second place finisher (a high school kid who was very nice after the race) to come over. Apparently the kid is a 17 year old from Chevy Chase, MD and has run many of the Celiac races around the country. Even more impressive – he has won most of the races he has entered. So they could have had a great story (the winner being a kid with Celiacs) and I had to spoil the fun.

I never want to turn into one of those guys who are so addicted to victory that they find every opportunity for a "W." The most notorious guy like this lives in Northern Virginia. His most repulsive victory was in a mile track race. Allegedly, he outkicked a 12-year-old girl and then pumped his fist Tiger Woods style after he crossed the finish line. Not that I'm anywhere close to being that bad – but today made me ponder how dark that part of me might be. I don't feel "awesome" about the race – but I do feel kinda good. Is that a bad thing?

Well, now that I got my competitive itch scratched – I'm going to try to keep to easy miles for most of the month of May. But who am I kidding – I'm not making any promises.

SUNDAY, MAY 10, 2009
THE SEASON OF LAZINESS

Today I was supposed to run – but I didn't. No, I wasn't injured or sick. I took 10 paces out the door this morning and said – "forget it." Kendra and I then went on an unplanned trip to Philly (note: the Eastern State Penitentiary is more interesting than Alcatraz). We came home I put on my running clothes and again took 10 steps out the door and just didn't feel it. I went to the fridge, grabbed a beer and chilled. I actually felt a slight twinge of guilt – but then I thought – to everything (turn, turn, turn) there is a season – and the season right now is the season of laziness.

I remember that my college coach used to say that the best runners are lazy. Not lazy in relation to a lot of people – but they are able to just chill. Runners who are always on the go rarely perform well. The body needs rest. Jim Adam, owner of Falls Road Running, likes to tell a story about an area runner who ran his best race the week after coming down with the flu. The forced bed rest had actually been good for him – of course when he felt better he started training too much again and never ran quite as fast ever again.

Three weeks ago I ran the Boston Marathon – but more importantly I ended a 24 week training cycle that was unlike anything I've put myself through in my life. By June I'll be running track workouts and from the end of June until the end of September I'll be running 70-90 miles per week, with three hard days (or two hard days and a race) per week. Now it's time to rest and be okay with being lazy.

MONDAY, MAY 18, 2009
MINE THAT BIRD

Yes – the filly horse did win this last weekend, and pretty much from beginning to end. But even more exciting to me was how Mine that Bird ended up second after being at the back of the pack again. I was ready to give all credit to the jockey for the Derby win – but the fact that Mine that Bird ran a pretty similar race with a different jockey shows that the instincts of the horse play a role as well.

There are times that horse racing seems somewhat cruel – but after watching these two races it's easy to think that Mine that Bird actually enjoys mixing it up down the stretch as much as we enjoy watching him. I was actually watching the race from a reception that proceeded a lecture by the author Michael Pollan. He wrote "Omnivore's Dilemma" and "In Defense of Food." One of his more interesting arguments is that our food system works best when we let a cow be a cow and a carrot be a carrot. There are natural systems that have developed over millions of years – including our relationships with other animals. We need to respect those systems or else we end up with weaker and less sustainable planet. The problem, Pollan argues, is our hubris in thinking that we can improve upon natural systems. We can't – and whenever we try nature eventually punches us in the gut to remind us who's boss.

I'm probably the millionth person to say this – but running is a great sport because it is so completely natural. We are all runners on some level – the design of our bodies is related to this one activity more than anything else. The same is true of horses – which is (along with my wife's favorite activity of low stakes gambling) why horse races can be so compelling. When we watch a horse race – we are seeing another animal doing something very natural and at the highest level possible.

When you run, especially against another person, you are recreating an event that has happened since the birth of our species. We all have the instinctual part of our brains that knew what it was to run with animals now long extinct. When you are able to access that place – running stops being a chore and becomes thrilling.

MONDAY, MAY 25, 2009
THE MAD SCIENTIST

A few days ago, I was reading about Mary Shelly's "Frankenstein." It was both the first modern horror story and the first science fiction story. Written in 1818 – it touched on many concepts that would not really be fully explored by literature or science for another century.

Probably the most obvious lesson of "Frankenstein" is the importance of airing out our wonderful ideas with others. This is as important when building a training plan as building a humanoid made from cadaver's body parts.

I'm not saying that you should always bend to what others say – you know your own body better than anybody else – but by this point pretty much every possible training strategy has been tried. If you don't use what others have learned, you are basically wasting your time – but at least you won't find yourself holed up in a dark castle waiting for the townsfolk with torches and pitchforks. It is, after all, just running.

ABOUT THE AUTHOR

Ben Ingram lives in Omaha, Nebraska with his wife Kendra. He is currently a student at University of Nebraska Medical Center in the Physician Assistant program. When he's not studying he's planning his next racing adventure.

www.ingramcontent.com/pod-product-compliance
Lightning Source LLC
Chambersburg PA
CBHW060327050426
42449CB00011B/2686